DOORS
to lock and
DOORS
to open

And I will give you the keys of the Kingdom of Heaven;
whatever doors you lock on earth shall be locked in heaven;
and whatever doors you open on earth shall be open in heaven!

—Matthew 16:19 (TLB)

The Discerning People of God

DOORS
to lock and
DOORS
to open

Leland Harder

Library of Congress Cataloging-in-Publication Data
Harder, Leland. 1926-
    Doors to lock and doors to open : the discerning people of God / Leland
Harder.
        p. cm.
        Companion vol. to: The Mennonite mosaic / J. Howard Kauffman. c1991.
        Includes bibliographical references.
        ISBN 0-8361-3628-4
        1. Sociology, Christian (Mennonite) 2. Mennonites—Doctrines.
3. Brethren in Christ Church—Doctrines. 4. Church and social problems—
Mennonites. 5. Church and social problems—Brethren in Christ Church.
I. Kauffman, J. Howard, 1919-   Mennonite mosaic. II. Title.
BX8121.2.H37 1993
289.7'73—dc20   93-10655
                                                                      CIP

All Scripture quotations are used by permission, all rights reserved, and unless
otherwise noted are from the *New Revised Standard Version Bible*, copyright 1989,
by the Division of Christian Education of the National Council of the Churches of
Christ in the USA; RSV from the Revised Standard Version of the Bible,
copyright 1946, 1952, 1971 by the Division of Christian Education of the National
Council of the Churches of Christ in the USA; TLB from *The Living Bible* © 1971
owned by assignment by Illinois Regional Bank N.A. (as trustee), used by
permission of Tyndale House Publishers, Inc., Wheaton, IL 60189; NEB from *The
New English Bible*. © The Delegates of the Oxford University Press and the Syndics
of the Cambridge University Press 1961, 1970.

DOORS TO LOCK AND DOORS TO OPEN
Copyright © 1993 by Herald Press, Scottdale, Pa. 15683
    Published simultaneously in Canada by Herald Press,
    Waterloo, Ont. N2L 6H7. All rights reserved
Library of Congress Catalog Number: 93-10655
International Standard Book Number: 0-8361-3628-4
Printed in the United States of America
Cover and book design by Paula M. Johnson

1 2 3 4 5 6 7 8 9 10 99 98 97 96 95 94 93

To Bertha
who in our forty years
of partnership has taught me much
about locking and opening doors

Contents

Foreword

IT IS A PLEASURE to introduce *Doors to Lock and Doors to Open,* a volume that offers excellent possibilities for Christian education settings as well as individual study and reflection. Here is a book that will help church members sink their teeth into some highly relevant topics, including the pressing question of how congregations make decisions affecting their participants.

This book is rooted in the belief that congregational participants need to grapple with issues much more profound than preparing and passing an annual budget (important as that is). The author assumes that it is the business of every congregation to determine what beliefs and practices to encouraged and which to discourage. The issue is which doors to open and which to close, as suggested in Matthew 16:19. Members are to be active participants in discernment—not just passive observers of Sunday worship services.

Is your congregation tradition-bound or open to change? Do the members seek to relate biblical principles to the issues of the day—such as individualism (chapter 8), peacemaking (chapter 11), political issues (chapter 12), women's roles in the church (chapter 10), abortion, homosexuality, and capital punishment (chapter 13)? How do members deal with differences of opinion (chapter 1)? Are they interested in cooperation between denominations (chapter 2)?

How would you classify your congregation—separatist, conservative, liberal, or transformist? Leland Harder explores these church types through the fascinating reports of persons he interviewed. Congregations come to life through the testimonies of real members.

The book had its origin in the 1989 survey of members of five Mennonite and Brethren in Christ denominations, the major findings of which were published in *The Mennonite Mosaic* (Herald Press, 1991), which I coauthored with Leo Driedger. When the administrative committee of that denominational survey project (called Church Member Profile II) considered how the findings should be reported, it accepted Harder's proposal to write a companion volume.

Harder's goal was to merge some of the survey results with a focus on nitty-gritty issues in congregational life. His proposal has now come to fruition. Those of us involved with the survey project heartily commend the book to individuals and groups for study and reflection on what it means to be God's servants in our churches and communities.

We are fortunate to have a person of Harder's training and experience to prepare this volume. Having been pastor in a number of congregations, he sees the issues from the inside. Having taught practical theology at the Associated Mennonite Biblical Seminaries (Elkhart, Ind.), Harder also has the insights of an educator. As researcher and associate director, he was deeply involved in both the 1972 and 1989 Mennonite church member surveys and was coauthor of *Anabaptists Four Centuries Later* (Herald Press, 1975), which reported on the 1972 survey results. He has the conviction that research results should be used not only by scholars and church leaders but by lay people as well.

The thirteen chapters of this book will fit nicely into a three-month series of Sunday school lessons, or weekly fellowship of Bible study groups. Each chapter ends with meaty discussion questions which focus the issues raised in the chapter. If used conscientiously, *Doors to Lock and Doors to Open* will make a significant contribution to the vitality of our congregations.

> —*J. Howard Kauffman, Director*
> *Church Member Profile II*
> *Goshen College, Goshen, Indiana*

Author's Preface

When it is evening, you say, "It will be fair weather, for the sky is red."
And in the morning, "It will be stormy today, for the sky is red and threatening."
You know how to interpret the appearance of the sky,
but you cannot interpret the signs of the times.
—Matthew 16:2-3

DISCERNING THE WEATHER on the basis of objective observations is a simple form of scientific knowledge. Discerning the "signs of the times" on the basis of objective observations of persons and groups was the purpose of the Church Member Profile (CMP) research project. CMP refers to a comprehensive study of the members of five Mennonite and Brethren in Christ denominations conducted in 1972 and again in 1989. At both times, over 3,000 members responded to a questionnaire probing from sixteen (1972) to nineteen (1989) areas of faith, life, attitudes, and behavior. Members gathered in their own congregational settings to fill out the questionnaires under direction of a trained research visitor.

The project was jointly sponsored by the five denominations and implemented by an administrative committee of official representatives of the five groups plus the research directors. It had three basic purposes: 1. to gather information that would be useful to denominational agencies planning their program agenda; 2. to gather data concerning the relationships between various demographic characteristics and the responses of members to all our questions; and 3. to interpret some of the main findings of the study in a more popular format for use in adult study groups in the churches, so members whose views were studied could be more involved in discerning the "signs of the times" in response to Christ's teachings.

This book that follows is our attempt to fulfill the third purpose of the

CMP research project. Readers who want to know more about the CMP research approach and findings are invited to consult the published volumes of Kauffman/Harder (1975) and Kauffman/Driedger (1991).

It is not as easy to discern the signs of the times in Christ's kingdom as to discern the face of the sky, but that is what we are called to do as members of Christ's church. In the chapters that follow, we will examine the congregational setting, biblical mandate, and social process of discernment in the church. In chapter 1 four typical members of four types of churches identify current questions they and their congregations are facing. They also indicate difficulties they are having in resolving issues. Excerpts from their interviews are inserted into every chapter to help readers make connections between issues discussed in this book and attitudes of representative church members.

One issue is the question of cooperation and integration between the participating denominations, discussed in chapter 2. Chapters 3-5 present the New Testament foundations for spiritual discernment, first in relation to the teachings of Jesus, then in relation to the authority of the Scriptures, and, third, in the perspective of the Jerusalem Conference (Acts 15).

In chapters 6-13, we pursue the discernment of Christ's initial and continuing call to faith, sorting out how faith forms and matures, who we are and what we believe, the pros and cons of individualistic faith, and the rewards and frustrations of corporate faith. We will probe two issues in the church's ministry—the elusive partnership between pastors and members and the roles of women and men.

Finally we will explore aspects of the high call of discipleship—how to be Christ's peacemakers in a world of violence, make political decisions as Christians, and discern other central issues of being Christians in our chaotic age. Out of the myriad of questions faced by churches today, three—abortion, capital punishment, and homosexuality—have been selected as case studies to illustrate the process for addressing the other issues as well. A Christ-centered model of decision making—the key to the kingdom of heaven!—is outlined as a climax to the book.

In writing this book, I walked a tightrope between my discipline as a social scientist and my calling as a Christian churchman. Some social scientists might criticize ways my theological biases have colored my sociological interpretations. And from the other side of the tightrope, some church members will lament my mixing biblical theology with sociology.

From the beginning of our planning to update the 1972 Church Member Profile, I was determined to write a study book for the churches. I'm grateful to the CMP Administrative Committee for consenting to my proposal, and I'm indebted to Leo Driedger, committee chairperson, for taking my place in the writing of *The Mennonite Mosaic* (the sequel to our earlier sociological work, *Anabaptists Four Centuries Later*).

In the writing of each chapter I had three kinds of objectives, suggested by the Mennonite Publishing House Foundation Series editors for their writers. There was

> 1. *a knowledge objective,* to give readers ideas and concepts based on Scripture, church history, and practical theology
> 2. *a feeling objective,* to help readers develop certain attitudes about Christ's commission to his church to be interpreters of the signs of the times and discerners of right and wrong, truth and error
> 3. *an action objective,* to move readers from relative uninvolvement in the discernment process to participation.

As a teaching aid for use in adult study groups, discussion questions are added at the end of each chapter. Scripture references are taken from the New Revised Standard Version unless otherwise indicated. The non-biblical references are identified in the text of each chapter by author and page numbers, with the title of the article or book listed at the end.

J. Howard Kauffman, director of the CMP research project, was especially helpful in running my computer printouts and rechecking my percentages for accuracy.

I gratefully acknowledge a generous research grant from the Schowalter Foundation, Inc., William L. Friesen, president and manager.

My special thanks go to Michael A. King, book editor for Herald Press, for his patient and supportive guidance of the manuscript through the process of acceptance for publication, editing, and revision.

Finally, I'm grateful to the members of my family who encouraged me to write this book after I had formally retired from a long academic career. Drawing on ideas and insights accumulated from twenty-five years of seminary teaching has made working on this project rewarding. The process almost led me to believe Reuel Howe's supposition that retirement really can be the commencement of "the creative years."

—*Leland Harder, Associate Director,*
Church Member Profile Research Project

PART A

The Meaning
and Process
of Discernment

CHAPTER 1

Church Member Profiles and Christian Discernment

Therefore, my brothers and sisters . . . stand firm in the Lord. . . .
I urge Euodia and I urge Syntyche to be of the same mind in the Lord.
Yes, and I ask you also, my loyal Syzygus, help these women,
for they have struggled beside me in the work of the gospel.
—Philippians 4:1-3

IN HIS LETTER TO THE CHURCH AT PHILIPPI, Paul wanted to help his fellow Christians discern the mind of Christ and what it meant to live on earth as citizens of Christ's kingdom. We don't know the specific disagreement between Euodia and Syntyche, but their quarrel concerned Paul because both were dear friends and active members of this beloved congregation. Paul admonished them to resolve their differences and called on Syzygus to help them to agree in the Lord.

Discernment is a popular word right now among church leaders and writers, but it is not a familiar term to many church participants. Jesus said that we are adept at discerning the face of the sky but cannot discern the signs of the times (Matt. 16:3). A *discerner* is an interpreter who arrives at a reasoned judgment on any matter involving truth or untruth. As a mandate given to the church (see chapter 3), discernment is a corporate process of sorting out some matter of controversy, seeking a solution to some problem, resolving some conflict, or finding an answer to some question.

Discernment is what the Church Member Profile research project is all about. A questionnaire of over 300 probes was administered to over 3,000 members. Twenty-two of those questioned returned for an oral interview about why they answered certain questions as they did. According to criteria defined in chapter 2, the attitudes of all persons interviewed were grouped and labeled as separatist (six persons), conservative (seven), liberal (four), and transformist (five). In this book each group will speak as one person with a fictitious name and place of resi-

17

dence. Thus each of the following four typical respondents is a composite of multiple interviews of persons representing similar points of view.

Four Typical Respondents

1. *Sally Mae Stauffer.* Asked whether she enjoyed answering the questionnaire, Sally Mae replied, "Yes, I did. I told my husband I couldn't begin to recall half of all the things that were asked."

I expressed appreciation for her willingness to answer questions, commenting on the fact that this was the first church assigned to me in which everyone who had fallen into our sample came.

"Oh," she replied, "I didn't know I could squirm out of it. Our minister had the impression from your letter that there could be no substitutes, and he told us to be there."

We laughed and I said, "I hope it wasn't quite that compulsory."

Sally Mae belongs to the Maple Creek Mennonite Church located in the open country north of Perrysburg. It is a separatist-type congregation (according to the chapter 2 classifications). The congregation is separatist in part because the average score of Maple Creek members on our separatism scale was higher than the average score for all persons responding to our survey. Sally Mae, for instance, strongly agrees that "Christians should avoid involvements in the 'kingdom of this world' as much as possible." Nevertheless, their church out in the country is about the only place Sally and her husband can really separate themselves from the "world," because they live in Perrysburg amidst all its residents.

Sally Mae is fifty-eight, married since age twenty-one, and living with her original spouse. Together they have belonged to the same denomination and congregation for all of these thirty-seven years. They raised a family of four children, none of whom now live nearby, and they have seven grandchildren whom they feel lucky to see once or twice a year.

A high school graduate, Sally Mae has no income-earning occupation, although she helps her husband administer an apartment house in Perrysburg that he purchased ten years ago as a supplemental source of future retirement income. The mortgage will be paid off in two more years—when her husband reaches his sixty-fifth birthday.

Here Sally Mae describes her church.

> Most members know each other intimately. When people in my church have economic need, most members give generously. Although most members make independent life decisions, there are certain expectations and standards by which everyone lives—and we all know what they are. When a church member is clearly guilty of an attitude or act that is sinful by the church's standards, he or she is usually confronted by the minister and asked to repent, although this used to happen more often than now. Many

of our young people have moved away and those who are left are the faithful few. We try to take seriously the apostle Paul's admonition not to be unequally yoked together with unbelievers (2 Cor. 6:14).

Sally Mae told about the teenage daughter of an elder in the church who ran away from home and was "unequally yoked" with an occult group engaged in Satan worship. When she came home weeks later, the girl was confused, and her parents took her to a Mennonite psychiatric center. During that time she lived in a group home run by Mennonites who belonged to a Christian charismatic fellowship.

Then the daughter returned to Perrysburg, got a job as a secretary in a drug rehabilitation agency, and lived at home with her parents. She seemed to be a changed person and volunteered to work with the Maple Creek Church young people, for whom she had a deep concern. The minister was afraid to let her do it. She had told him that since receiving the baptism of the Holy Spirit, she'd been empowered to resist the lures of Satan and wanted to help others of her age do so also.

She had a new love for her home church and liked the singing of old hymns *a cappella*, but she wished people would allow some guitar accompaniment, learn to compose some of their own songs, and be freer to worship God through the direct leading of the Holy Spirit.

I asked Sally Mae whether the members of the congregation had discussed the girl's proposals. "No," she said, "the minister and elders make most of the decisions, and they decided it would be best if the elder's daughter found another Mennonite church where she would feel at home, perhaps one with a charismatic form of worship."

I wondered how Sally Mae had answered the questionnaire item that asked whether the charismatic movement had benefited the Mennonite Church. She was undecided but added that after the return of the elder's daughter, the members were about equally divided on this question, although nobody wanted to argue with the minister and elders. The elder's daughter was suggesting changes, and most of the people wanted to keep things as they were.

Sally Mae herself is uncertain about all of this but tends to keep her thoughts to herself. The congregation has been studying the book of Acts in their midweek meeting at church and recently studied Acts 19, where Paul arrived at Ephesus and asked the believers whether or not they had received the Holy Spirit when they believed. They replied, "No, we haven't even heard that there is a Holy Spirit."

Sally Mae thought of the elder's daughter, and the minister's explanation of this passage didn't fully satisfy her curiosity, for he had said only that it's not possible to be a disciple of Christ and not know the Holy Spirit. Sally Mae wondered what the people of her church would say if

Paul asked them that same question, but she was afraid to speak up at the meeting.

Although she has unspoken reservations about how decisions are made in a separatist church like hers, she is deeply committed to the people at Maple Creek, their leaders, and their way of trying to be obedient to the teachings of the Bible. She strongly feels that the Mennonite vision of a "glorious church, not having spot, or wrinkle" (Eph. 5:27, KJV) is a wonderful heritage that has given them an awareness of the conditions for maintenance of a separate and holy way of life. However fashionable it may have become to criticize such withdrawal from the ways of the world, for Maple Creek members separation offers a secure context for living the Christian life.

2. *Glenn Klassen.* My wife and I joined Glenn and his wife for dinner in a local restaurant. The interview began over dessert and continued afterward at their home. When Glenn referred to his reticence in the company of authority figures, I asked whether it had been hard to agree to this conversation with us.

He replied, "I didn't know I had to do this. Our minister said only that we were to meet you for dinner, but it was just as well that I got caught up in the conversation before I knew what was happening. I'm really enjoying this!"

At age forty-six, Glenn farms the land his great-grandfather purchased from the Chicago and Northwestern Railroad when he immigrated from Russia in 1875. Glenn is the fourth generation of Klassens on the farm.

To the question, "What's new about farming today?" he replied,

> Mostly the expenses, and the reason is this: You've got to farm much more land to make it, use more chemicals, more machinery, more of everything, all of which has to be paid for at the end of the year. Then if you don't get much for your product, it's hard to do. You almost always have to borrow from the bank for one thing or another. The tractor my father bought new for $8,500 now sells for $50,000 to $60,000. A new combine lists for $93,000. Seed corn costs about $25 an acre, and your fertilizer is another $40. The higher your yield, the more you flood the market. All of a sudden corn sells for $1.50. That doesn't pay for a combine, I'll tell you!
>
> Then your wife goes to work and you rent additional land. We farm 700 acres now, and even that's not considered big farming. It's a lot of work, but you've got to do it to make it. There's a sense in which this recent drought is the best thing that's happened, because we're getting rid of the surplus. Sometimes we make more money in our dry years than in our wet years. If everybody gets rain, you're going to see corn sell for a buck and a half again; but if it stays dry, you might get half a crop but the price doubles. You can make just as much and you don't have the surplus. Then after a couple of good years, the bins are full and we're in trouble again.

Whatever business you're in, you can hang in there only so many years without making money. I might have quit in '85 or '86 when we were hitting bottom, except for the fact that my wife had an income and I'm doing what I love to do. When I got out of school, I got a job in town, waiting for something better to open up. My chance came when my dad retired. Frankly, I feel God called me to be a farmer, just like he called our minister to be a preacher. I really think a Christian in any job should be able to fulfill a Christian calling, and God wouldn't call you to do something you wouldn't enjoy or that you're not capable of doing. Not everyone can be a preacher, and not everyone can be a farmer.

Glenn and his wife are members of the Spring Valley Mennonite Brethren Church located in the town of Midland. It is a conservative-type church, in part because the average score of their participant members on our conservatism scale was higher than average. In the American political arena, for instance, Glenn is most in agreement with the Republican Party conservatives and voted for George Bush in 1988, as did most members of his church.

Glenn strongly agrees the Bible is the divinely inspired and inerrant Word of God and that Jesus was not only human but also divine—and he has no doubts about these beliefs. His church has over 400 members and he says that most members know only about a fourth of the other members intimately. There is little mutual consultation about how members live, and Jesus is seen more as the personal Savior who died for our sins than as the suffering servant who calls us to follow his example.

I asked Glenn about his answers to questions probing his involvement in the local church. He serves as an usher occasionally and on the refreshment committee with his wife. Otherwise he shies away from church leadership because he freezes up when expected to speak in a group.

He explains these inhibitions by referring to the class distinctions that have always characterized his church. For years the business people and town people were the leaders, but the farmers were never a part of the in-group here. They were looked upon as a bunch of dummies. When Glenn was in high school and told his friends he wanted to farm, they thought he was crazy. It's less that way now since farming has become an agribusiness—and even a profession after some of the younger generation graduated from the university with a degree in agricultural economics and came back home to farm.

I asked Glenn whether his church had ever planned a public discussion of the plight of farmers in the community, and he said no. He doubts the church could do much to help farmers in their times of crisis except pray for them. He was lucky in not being forced to buy more land to survive. Able to rent land, he didn't have to go into as much debt as the younger farmers. He believes his conservative farming practices have been an important factor. He tries to avoid loans he isn't sure he could handle. He couldn't easily live with a great amount of debt when measured by what he calls the asset-to-debt ratio.

Glenn feels his survival on the farm has been due more to his membership in the Farm Management Association (FMA) than his membership in the Spring Valley Church. FMA is an extension of the state agricultural college. Tax work and farm-related decisions are examined with a farm management specialist, and Glenn believes this has helped him understand and apply the asset-to-debt ratio.

Glenn believes, however, that the church could be of greater help with the moral-ethical side of farming. He explained,

> You know that the moral aspects of farming are changing when your neighbor starts to plug your tiles or tries to raise the cash rate on you when you bid for rented land. That's not family farming, that's just plain selfishness and greed. Last winter I rented a farm on which a neighbor and church member was also bidding. I knew there was a low spot that needed tiling. So I tiled it and planted in spring. Then we had some rains and the field wasn't draining. I talked to my neighbor and told him I was going to get the owner out there to help me investigate.
>
> A week later, after more rain, the field was completely drained, and I knew my neighbor had plugged and unplugged it. I talked to the guy who tiled it, and he told me exactly where the tile went into my neighbor's land and drained into his creek, where he had the perfect opportunity to plug it with rocks.
>
> When things like this happen, you know it's getting to be a crooked business. The competition is so great that farmers are tempted to cheat and human relationships are affected. It's hard to believe that someone can go to church on Sunday and plug a neighbor's tiles on Monday, just because he was angry that he didn't get the rental land.

I told Glenn that Jesus had the solution to a problem like that. According to Matthew 18, if brothers or sisters sin against you, go to them and talk about it. If they confess and repent, you have regained fellowship. If not, take along another brother or sister, and the three of you discuss it. If that doesn't bring reconciliation, then take the matter to the entire church.

Glenn said he would be willing to do that if he had any confidence the church would be there, ready to get involved in the process. He doubts, however, that following Matthew 18 is still a possibility in our churches. Church members are so individualistic they don't let the church get involved in their private affairs. Glenn said he gets more guidance for handling some problems when he drinks coffee with his friends in town. "That's never time wasted," he commented. "I often learn from somebody else's experience."

Another issue Glenn would like to see discussed in church is working on Sunday.

> We were brought up to believe we shouldn't work on Sunday. We worked six days a week, and after early Sunday chores, we went to church and relaxed the rest of the day. Now there are more and more church members who work on Sunday, including the guy who plugged my tile.
>
> I think all of this started when he began to work on Sunday. Then everything started going downhill for him, and he's never been the same since. When he felt he had to start working on Sunday, I asked our pastor to preach a sermon on the fourth commandment, and the pastor asked me why, when I pick corn on Sunday. I said I don't pick corn on Sunday.
>
> Then the pastor said, "But I'll bet you have your drier running."
>
> I said, "No, we were taught at home to shut it off for Sunday."
>
> He replied, "But how do you know that is the right thing to do? Maybe it's not wrong to dry corn on Sunday." He referred to the ox falling into the ditch on the Sabbath.
>
> I said, "Yes, but if it repeatedly falls into the ditch, maybe you should get rid of the ox or fill in the ditch."

Glenn wonders whether the church has changed its teaching about Matthew 18 and the Ten Commandments, and whether the authority of the Scriptures which we affirm in principle can really be experienced in practice. "Otherwise, you begin to feel like you're crazy to try to keep the Sabbath and to live according to the teachings of Jesus to love God with all your heart and to love your neighbor as yourself."

3. *Denise Preheim.* It was easy to engage in conversation with Denise because she had been my seminary student in the mid-'70s. She graduated with an M.Div. degree, fully prepared to enter pastoral ministry but found no openings. Now at age thirty-eight she answered "Yes" to the questions "Do you believe that women in Canadian and American societies are being discriminated against and denied certain basic rights?" and "Should the policy in your denomination allow for the ordination of women to the Christian ministry?" She expressed continuing resentment that even the churches in her more liberal denomination were still so closed to the idea of women in pulpit ministry.

After seminary graduation, Denise entered a clinical pastoral education program and was certified as a hospital chaplain. After six years of chaplaincy in Wichita and five years as a therapist at a mental health center, she went into private practice as a therapist with a professional psychologist. Their speciality is a concept of wholistic therapy that tries to integrate faith as defined by the client with emerging new self-awareness and self-direction.

Denise belongs to the Prince of Peace Mennonite Church in West Newton and has been active as a leader in various roles—the peace and social concerns commission, the staff advisory committee, and the church council. Her church has been classified as liberal. She identifies her political position as "Democratic Party liberal" and voted for Michael Dukakis in 1988. On the subject of cooperation between churches of different denominations, Denise believes every effort should be made toward more integration of denominational and congregational programs. She recently served on the joint committee that published a new peace-church hymnal. One of her roles on that committee was to help the hymnal reflect concerns about sexist language.

Denise describes her church as Christ-centered but open to diverse interpretations of what that means in life situations. In principle, she and most members of her church see Jesus more as the suffering servant who calls us to follow his example than as the personal Savior who died for our sins. Most members make independent decisions about how they live their lives and feel it is more important to work for a just and equitable world than to help individuals find a personal saving faith.

On the question of frequency of church attendance, Denise hedged, checking "once or twice a month." She explained,

> Occasionally I'm out of town, and occasionally I have to see a client on Sunday morning. I might be out of town for a conference or what not. I suppose I could say that except for the times I have a professional conflict, I go to church almost every week. I haven't been involved in a Sunday school class yet, though I intend to do so. I consider attending Sunday worship essential to my well-being and ability to function in my vocation as a faith-centered therapist. It's one of those things I do like eating and sleeping—it's central.

Denise also hedged a bit on the question "How close do you describe your present relationship to God?" checking "between distant and close." She noted,

> I have a great respect for God. I used to not have. I used to blame God for things, like the incredible words of Paul about keeping women silent in the church. But I don't do that anymore. I learned the hard way that when you try to make things come out right by yourself and you're not respecting God as transcending all human foibles, God lets you hurt until you learn. I think it's kind of irreverent not to fear God a little, as the ancient Hebrews wrote in their wisdom literature. I hear born-again Christians say things like "God is my copilot" or "God is my best friend," and I recoil at the implication that they are on God's level. I think of God as both love and justice, and I pray to God on both levels.

Denise believes God has been revealed in the person of Jesus Christ and that in Christ we have a remarkably clear vision of how we are to live in God's kingdom. It is up to us as Christians to try continually to discern what is required of us to follow Christ in particular situations and in relation to particular needs in society. She said, "I felt some of us were doing that when we had our weekly noon-hour prayer vigil in front of the court house during the Persian Gulf War."

On the question of what she believes about the Bible, she checked "I believe that the Bible is the authoritative Word of God and a reliable guide, but it is not inerrant." She sees no contradiction between affirming the authority of the Bible and observing its authorship by fallible humans like Paul, who admitted in 1 Corinthians 7 that sometimes he couldn't say that his teaching came from the Lord, but he was giving his opinion nevertheless, always wanting to test everything and to hold fast to what is right (1 Thess. 5:21).

Denise wishes that her church could be more unified in its corporate witness in the community and in the world, and that more members would be more socially concerned about issues like sexual abuse, violence on TV, militarism, unemployment, and poverty. She believes the congregation's peace and social concerns commission is seriously working on some of this agenda, but her unresolved question is how to get more members engaged in the discernment process.

As a small step in that direction, she is looking forward to Peace Emphasis Sunday, when the commission will be in charge of the worship service and present some of its agenda to the congregation. At the same time she is sobered by the thought that we spend so much time talking and so little trying to change things in our society. Her vision of the Christian life is the interplay of corporate discernment at church and specific engagement with the problems confronting us in the world.

4. *Menno Isaac.* Our fourth interview began with the occupational question. "I'm a professional," said Menno. "I work as an engineer."

At age twenty-seven, Menno has a degree in ceramic engineering from Waterloo University. He deals with materials—organic, inorganic, and metallic. He is currently employed by Honeywell at their solid-state electronics division in Hamilton, Ontario. Honeywell is involved in advancing the semiconductor industry, working with such aspects as solid-state computer chips and solid-state electronic devices.

Some of the output of Menno's division is for commercial products and some for military products. Some Honeywell sensors, for instance, are used in both civilian and military airplanes for determining the pitch of the plane, how fast it is rising, and wind speed. Menno's talent, and consequently his job, is to make the whole system work together so that it will meet the requirements of a reliable product. Thus he does a lot of things that go beyond his technical training.

Menno enjoys his work and is paid handsomely with an annual salary approaching six figures, but that only complicates the vocational dilemma he is facing. The charter of his division has been gradually shifting toward more support of the military. Because of his pacifist commitment, he is beginning to wonder how long he can work there. He was fortunate in the past to be allowed to select involvement in commercial rather than military programs.

Some of his departmental colleagues thought it was because he was the boss' favorite, but he made a good name for himself in whatever program he started and made a lot of money for the company. Consequently they gave him freedom to work on some of the more important programs in the facility—which had been the commercial ones. Now some of the more important programs are the huge military contracts coming from the United States. Already a year ago Menno turned down leading one of these programs because of his beliefs, and he doesn't know how long he can continue his antimilitary dissent without losing his job.

Menno grew up in a Mennonite church in Winnipeg and deeply appreciated the inter-Mennonite fellowship at Waterloo University. Upon moving to Hamilton, he and his new wife joined an inter-Mennonite Bible study group that subsequently evolved into a house church with membership in the dually-affiliated (MC and GCMC) Mennonite Conference of Eastern Canada. The name they chose for their church is Escarpment Anabaptist Fellowship, because they meet in a club house on the Escarpment in Hamilton. They prefer the New Testament term "fellowship" (*koinonia*) to "church" (*ecclesia*) because the former connotes a shared partnership in the gospel.

The Escarpment Fellowship has been classified in our study as a transformist-type church. Like the separatist type, these members tend to score high on the separatism scale. As Menno explains,

> There are two aspects to separatism for us. One is theological—we are separatist in believing in the doctrine of two worlds and making a clear distinction of which kingdom we belong to. The other is social—we're separate because as an Anabaptist-oriented house church we are nonconformist in our ethical commitments and lifestyle, even when we live and work in the structures of this world. It's not clear yet how hard it's going to be for us to move into society and function as Anabaptist Christians in our vocations, but certainly our basic congregational covenant can reinforce the separatist attitude—although we're not radical to the point of feeling like we have to build walls between ourselves and the rest of society.

The other criterion by which the Escarpment Fellowship has been classified as transformist is the welfare attitudes scale, on which members would be gauged as liberal-minded. In the 1988 national Canadian election, for instance, they tended to vote for the Liberal candidate, John Turner, or the New Democratic Party candidate, Edward Broadbent.

Although presently operating as a house church without a salaried pastor, the Fellowship is not opposed to having a paid pastor in the future. They haven't discussed that option much, but Menno is clear about one thing. If they hire a pastor, they will not want to give up their present pattern of shared ministry.

At present they are meeting twice a week, on Sunday morning and Wednesday evening, and sharing meals on both occasions. They serve as pastors to each other. Already they have grown from ten to twenty-eight members and may soon want to divide into two or more groups for Wednesday evening meetings. If they do that, they may soon need a kind of pastoral director to coordinate their activities and help plan and lead their Sunday morning worship and Bible study.

So far their meetings have centered on discussion of vital ethical issues in their lives in light of their corporate study of the Bible. They recently completed a study of the Sermon on the Mount, using John Miller's *The Christian Way*.

This study led to several discernments and decisions in the group. One was to clarify their peace witness, with particular reference to their vocations in the metropolitan city of Hamilton. Each member will share experiences in their current work situations in which the pacifist ethic of Jesus is being compromised and in which some form of more intentional witness is needed.

The other decision was to write a covenant of membership for their Fellowship to make their self-identity as a church more explicit. They are aware of the difficulties of living up to a perfectionist kind of covenant statement and of the sober prophecy of Jeremiah that because of the disobedience of the ancient covenant community, the coming Messiah would write his covenant upon their hearts (Jer. 31:31-35). They feel, however, that the Lord was in fact writing on their hearts as they studied his Sermon on the Mount, and now they believe they could be more accountable if they would covenant together in a more explicit way.

The members of Escarpment Anabaptist Fellowship believe the peace churches could have a much greater impact if they restructured congregations as ethically discerning communities of committed Christians. Their own mission, they believe, is to become an experimental model of such a church.

Different Conversations Within a Common Tradition

Sally Mae Stauffer, Glenn Klassen, Denise Preheim, and Menno Isaac represent attitudes more or less familiar to all of us. Although they are composite representations with fictitious names and places, the interpretations they voiced and the stories they told came from real persons. Two men and two women in their 20s, 30s, 40s, and 50s, they live on a farm, in a town, in a city, and in a large industrial urban center. The churches of which they are members represent four types—separatist, conservative, liberal, and transformist.

In the remaining chapters of this book, further excerpts from our interviews as filtered through the composite voices of these four representatives will be inserted to interpret their diverse attitudes on a number of discernment issues. Each time we will try to imagine the kind of discussion they would be having among themselves if they actually met.

Beneath their different points of view is a certain unity that tempers their diversity. First, they all belong to a common Anabaptist-Mennonite rootage and tradition. In chapters 6 and 7, we will probe further how their Christian identity has been formed and integrated, what it is, and what they believe.

Second, all four representatives have high views of the church as a fellowship of believers. They are committed members and attend regularly, not just out of habit but out of conviction. The church is obviously prominent in their lives, although they sense that there is a tension between their individualism as members and their commitment to a covenant discipline. This dilemma will be explored further in chapter 8.

Third, they all have high views of biblical authority. None had any problem describing the Bible as the authoritative Word of God and a reliable guide for faith and life. They differed only with respect to the use of *inerrant*, a term unacceptable to Denise and Menno. How we move from a doctrine of the Bible to use of the Bible as guide will be discussed in chapter 4.

Fourth, they all had a high Christology, and out of a list of statements describing five views of Jesus, they all affirmed both his humanity and deity. They differed only with respect to whether they still have doubts about the nature of Christ. How the teachings of Jesus about discipleship and the Holy Spirit can change our lives and make us more mature followers will be examined in chapters 3, 5, and 6.

Finally, and most significant for the central theme of our book, they all affirmed the importance of ongoing corporate discernment of issues in the life of the church. Whether or not they admitted to doubts about the Christian faith, they all sensed gaps and lags in the living of the faith. Their high view of biblical authority is a constant reminder that in their personal and corporate discernment of the mind of Christ on particular issues, they actually do so little with the Bible as "a trustworthy guide for faith and life."

Their high view of Jesus as Lord is a constant reminder that he is always up ahead, beckoning us to follow in his steps. They realize that in their daily decisions about many things, they really hardly know how to ask the question with which we began this chapter: "What is the mind of Christ on the particular issue we're facing?"

Thus all four persons with whom we conversed believe that we still have much to learn about what it should mean to us to say that the Bible is God's Word and that God's Son Jesus is Lord.

Discussion Questions

1. Are the four members described in this chapter represented in the membership of your church? If your congregation tends to have a predominance of one of the four types (separatist, conservative, liberal, transformist), which type is it?

2. Despite their differences, do Sally, Glenn, Denise, and Menno have a common Anabaptist-Mennonite tradition? A common view of the church as a fellowship of believers? A common view of the Bible as the authoritative guide for faith and life?

3. What did the apostle Paul write in Philippians 4:1-3 about how persons like Sally Mae and Denise should deal with differences? Does that work in your church?

4. What do you think about how Sally Mae's church responded to the proposals of the elder's daughter? Would your church have responded differently?

5. Could the Matthew 18 teaching have been used effectively to resolve Glenn's accusations against his neighbor? In his attitude about not working on Sunday, is Glenn just being a legalist or is he trying to practice a vital biblical principle?

6. When Denise graduated from seminary and wanted to be a pastor, was she really victimized by unchristian attitudes prejudicial to women in our churches?

7. In his pacifist protests at Honeywell, is Menno being too radical at the risk of losing his job? Or is he doing what all of us should be doing wherever we live and work?

CHAPTER 2

Church Types as Discernment Environments

Let anyone who has an ear listen to what
the Spirit is saying to the churches.
—Revelation 2:7, 11, 17, 29; 3:6, 13, 22

THIS REFRAIN WAS SUNG SEVEN TIMES to specific churches in Asia Minor. As described in John's Revelation, the churches were quite different and there was diversity within each one. Their members were variously described as faithful and faithless, repentant and unrepentant, poor and rich, Jewish and Gentile, fervent and lukewarm.

The Five Participating Denominations between CMP I and II

Like these seven churches, the five denominations participating in the Church Member Profile research project in 1973 and 1989 are alike in certain respects and different in others. In our CMP I book, *Anabaptists Four Centuries Later*, we used a phrase to summarize the distinctive identity of each group, but changes since then have obscured certain aspects and highlighted others. This can be illustrated by comparing the earlier and later groups on eight factors—discipleship, pacifism, evangelism, morality, church discipline, church unity, urbanization, and ethnicity.

The Mennonite Church (MC): Guardian of the Anabaptist Vision. The oldest and largest of the five groups is the only one whose name does not have a qualifying adjective. It is proud to be known simply as "The Mennonite Church." Harold Bender's admonition, "We must deliberately and consciously hold our own" (H. Bender, B, 47), was taken to heart.

Since then, according to George R. Brunk II, the MC has not been holding its own. "Although there was at one time a significant difference between these two groups [MC and GCMC], it appears now that they are traveling on essentially the same track of accommodation and compromise" (Brunk II, 9).

Our CMP data show that Brunk is right that MCs are now more similar to other Anabaptist groups, but he is not entirely correct in assuming this is due to accommodation and compromise. According to our eight measurements, the MC has lost a little ground on the probes of discipleship, pacifism, morality, and church discipline—but it has gained ground on the evangelism and church unity questions. Despite these changes, the distinctive MC identity as guardian of the Anabaptist vision remains intact. Brunk's son, George R. Brunk III, describes the MC as a denomination in which the historic Anabaptist doctrines of discipleship and discipline, nonresistance, and nonconformity are still taught and accepted (Brunk III, B, 840-2).

Nevertheless, the changes have been significant. Beulah Hostetler describes the interval between our CMP I and CMP II as "a time of reinterpretation, characterized by leadership and organizational adjustments to a changed reality." For example, communion is now served at General Assembly, signaling the demise of *close communion*, which "allowed only members in full fellowship to participate." This in turn "heralded the relaxation of discipline, which had been closely tied to the preparatory meeting which preceded close communion."

The plain coat for ministers and the head covering for women are disappearing. Musical instruments in worship are now commonplace, although some congregations still sing unaccompanied. "A return to congregational autonomy, with conferences being advisory" was authorized by a churchwide plan of reorganization. The traditional bishop-preacher-deacon pattern of leadership has been largely replaced by a professional pastor assisted by a board of elders or church council. Women are increasingly serving in ministry, and a few are being ordained as pastors (Hostetler, 565).

The General Conference Mennonite Church (GCMC): Progress Through Inter-Mennonite Cooperation. There were two facets to this image of the second largest Mennonite denomination. One was the identity of this progressive branch of Mennonites, which implied willingness to adopt methods of church work from others (such as the parliamentary process of decision making). The other idea was the emphasis on cooperation. The main goal formulated at the 1860 GCMC plan of organization through which GCMC was founded was to unite all Mennonites for the purposes of church renewal and mission to the world.

Among other Mennonite groups, these emphases conveyed the image of a liberal ecumenical church that tolerated heretical ideas and accommodated worldly behavior. To be sure, more emphasis was placed on inter-Mennonite cooperation than on uniformity of lifestyle. The GCMC motto was unity in essentials, liberty in nonessentials, and love in all things.

Mennonite Brethren historian Paul Toews notes that while MCs have pursued faithfulness by defining the boundaries and controlling who goes in and out, GCs have pursued faithfulness by defining the core convictions and letting the boundaries be fuzzy (quoted by Schlabach, 5). Liberty in matters like attire and forms of worship allow for wholesome diversity and wider inter-Mennonite unity.

According to our selective probes, the GCs have not been changing as much as the MCs in the interval between CMP I and II. While the shifts in the areas of pacifism and church discipline for MCs were in the direction of accommodation, the GC shifts in the same areas were in the direction of greater commitment to the historic peace position. On the pacifism probe, for instance, GC respondents selecting nonmilitary options increased from 65 to 67 percent while MC respondents decreased from 88 to 80 percent.

Under the contrasting influences of acculturation and recommitment, respectively, the two groups have been moving closer together, so that now, in sixteen of twenty-five measurements of faith, ethics, and ministry, they are positioned side by side when ranked with the other three groups (L. Harder, G, 9). Moreover, on ten of the measurements, they rank in first and second position, calling into question the judgment of Brunk II that the changes categorically indicate compromise and accommodation.

Meanwhile, the GCMC ranks first among the five groups on our composite ecumenicity scale. Its most distinctive features continue to be

> readiness to cooperate in many inter-Mennonite activities, congregational independence, diversity of thought and lifestyle, a free borrowing from outside Mennonite tradition, laxness in applying Christian discipline, a strong desire to remain biblical, yet recognizing that differences in hermeneutical approach to the Bible lead to differing interpretations of the Scriptures, a rediscovery and emphasis of a peace position, a constant attempt to keep evangelism and Christian education and nurture together, and a continued emphasis on church renewal. (Poettcker, 332)

The Mennonite Brethren Church (MBC): *Return to Menno and the Bible.* The MBC, the third largest group, originated as a renewal movement in South Russia emphasizing personal conversion, a return to the sixteenth-century Anabaptist reformer Menno Simons, and to the Bible as God's Word. The MBC was founded in 1860 as a radical corrective to moral lapse in the Russian Mennonite enclaves and to the failure to share the economic resources of the land.

Since then, the MBs have been more attracted to other evangelical groups than to other Mennonites. However, between CMP I and CMP II their interest in inter-Mennonite unity has gained some ground, as has their adherence to the Anabaptist norms of pacifism and church discipline. Conversely, commitments to discipleship and morality appear to be eroding slightly.

These shifts are related to demographic changes. MBs are no longer primarily a people of the land but are the most urbanized of the five groups. Consequently they are becoming more diversified ethnically and theologically. Three MB scholars interpreted some of the changes in the MBC as follows:

> There continued to be a strong affirmation of the doctrinal confession of the Mennonite Brethren church, with the exception of the peace position.
> While radical discipleship and peacemaking are central in our beliefs, there was little support for the promotion of peace, for practicing injustice among members, and for exercising church discipline.
> While greater ethnic diversity in the churches may be regarded positively as a result of greater involvement in the world, the implications for denominational identity require further reflection.
> Members expressed a stronger commitment to shared leadership but a decreased commitment to membership accountability.
> Respondents expressed positive political attitudes, but they were less supportive of specific political endorsements by the local congregation.
> In general, Mennonite Brethren expressed conservative attitudes in personal moral practices. (Toews/Konrad/Dueck, 23-24)

Brethren in Christ (BIC): *Synthesis of Anabaptism and Pietism.* The fourth participating denomination began in Pennsylvania about 1780. E. Morris Sider writes that

> the founders, largely of Anabaptist background (probably mainly Mennonite) were deeply influenced by the pietistic revival movement of the period which emphasized a crisis conversion experience, with an attendant belief in a personal "heartfelt" relationship to God. . . . During their first century the Brethren in Christ worked out a synthesis of their Anabaptist-pietistic beliefs. Their emphasis on a two-kingdom theology (nonconformity) made them one with other Anabaptist groups in such matters as nonresistance and nonparticipation in politics. They wore simple, or plain, clothing, and they practiced brotherhood, including such matters as church discipline and caring for one another. (E. Sider, 97)

Since 1972 the BICs have experienced many of the same changes as the MCs. They have experienced a decline in discipleship, pacifism, and morality. However, we measured serious BIC concern for church discipline and inter-Mennonite unity.

Evangelical Mennonite Church (EMC): Search for Self-Identity in the American Environment. The EMC is the Mennonite group that has experienced the greatest accommodation to the American social and religious environment and has offered the fewest identity guidelines for coping with environmental influences. EMC roots were in the nineteenth-century Amish church. But after one generation following the original schism, when the EMC clung to nonconforming traditions more conservative than its Amish roots, it began to borrow church-work methods from American revivalism and fundamentalism.

The EMCs' ethic was originally pacifist, as indicated by its original name—Defenseless Mennonite Church—but today less than 20 percent of its members are pacifist by our indicator, and it ranks lowest of the five denominations on discipleship, pacifism, church discipline, church unity, and ethnicity. Stan Nussbaum describes more recent developments.

> Since its origin in 1865 in Berne, Indiana, it has moved from its Amish roots through the middle of the Mennonite family and into the Evangelical portion of the North American spectrum. During the 30 years from 1955 to 1985, the denomination has continued to struggle to relate the "evangelical" and the "Mennonite" aspects of its name and heritage. (Nussbaum, 276)

Overall, a problem inherent in the Mennonite/BIC experience is that two of their most valued biblical norms seem to work at cross-purposes. As the following tabulation shows, there is an inverse correlation between the percentage of members recruited from non-Mennonite/non-BIC parentage (the evangelistic norm) and the percentage of members adhering to pacifism (the nonresistance norm).

	Rank Order	
	Percent of Members of Non-Mennonite Parents	Percent of Members Who Would Refuse Military Service
EMC	1	5
BIC	2	4
MBC	3	3
GCMC	4	2
MC	5	1

By the criterion of winning new members and establishing new churches, the EMC is the most successful of the five groups, but it is giving up on nonresistance. The planting of new churches has been so successful that over half of the present EMC membership belong to congregations less than thirty years old.

None of the new churches are in traditionally Mennonite communities; all of them have a heavy emphasis on personal conversion. The rapid growth of churches with such shallow Mennonite roots naturally affects the way the denomination as a whole sees itself. The trend is toward separating the concepts of church planting and the Mennonite heritage, giving priority to church planting. (Nussbaum, 278)

Diversity Within Each Denomination

In the earlier CMP study, we found many similarities among the five groups. Indeed, our common Anabaptist roots and our common commitment to mission and service have been the basis for cooperation in numerous inter-Mennonite agencies, like the Mennonite Central Committee (MCC), Mennonite Disaster Service (MDS), and the Africa Inter-Mennonite Mission (AIMM).

But some of our CMP II consultants felt that we had not given sufficient attention to Mennonite pluralism within the family of churches. Rodney Sawatsky was especially critical of our book, *Anabaptists Four Centuries Later*, for perpetuating the stereotype of a single normative Anabaptist vision when in fact there were multiple visions.

Sawatsky rejects the charge that "pluralism" among the Anabaptists means that they were "pluralists"—that is, that they believed there is more than one kind of ultimate truth. On the contrary, while their movement contained subgroups that were geographically separated and had different leaders and emphases, they were all struggling to discern the same ultimate truth (Sawatsky, 150-1). They were trying to be a discerning people of God under the lordship of Christ, moving toward consensus under the guidance of the Holy Spirit. That was their unity amidst their diversity.

Four Types of Congregation

Sawatsky created a diagram of present-day Anabaptist-Mennonite congregations along two dimensions

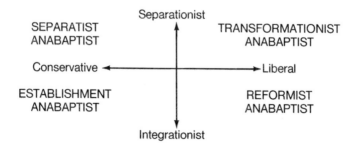

By calling all four types Anabaptist, Sawatsky rejected a single Anabaptist norm. The vertical dimension divides congregations between separationist and integrationist positions with respect to society in general, and other Christian denominations in particular. The separatist position suggests relative withdrawal from North American society. The integrationist position suggests relative harmony and commonality with North American society. (Sawatsky, 149-50)

The horizontal dimension divides the congregation between conservative and liberal attitudes with respect to political and ethical issues. Implicit in such indicators is a skepticism on the part of conservatives about governmental intervention in our lives. On the other hand, liberals tend to want to use national resources and leadership to resolve social-economic problems.

From the 333-item questionnaire administered to members of 153 congregations, it was not difficult to find appropriate "yardsticks" or measurements for the two dimensions of Sawatsky's classification. For the vertical dimension, five questions combined into a separatism scale were used (see Kauffman-Driedger, 91-92). For the horizontal dimension, three questions comprising a welfare attitudes scale were used (Kauffman-Driedger, 205). (Thirty-five churches that fell close to the mean of either dimension were deleted, leaving ninety-eight to represent the four types). For the sake of brevity, Sawatsky's labels were changed to

Type A, separatist: 29 churches, 542 member respondents
Type B, conservative: 26 churches, 507 member respondents
Type C, liberal: 22 churches, 452 member respondents
Type D, transformist: 21 churches, 441 member respondents

Of the 98 churches that fell into our classification, 34 are MC, 30 GCMC, 22 MBC, 9 BIC, and 3 EMC. Seventy are located in the United States and 28 in Canada. No typology like this is a perfect classification of the reality it tries to gauge. At best it is an experimental tool to aid and guide readers in further discernment of issues discussed in this book. The four types will be the basis for our examination of many kinds of questions.

The Question of Church Unity

Now I appeal to you, brothers and sisters, by the name of our Lord Jesus Christ, that all of you be in agreement and that there be no divisions among you. . . . For it has been reported to me . . . that each of you says, "I belong to Paul," or "I belong to Apollos," or "I belong to Cephas," or "I belong to Christ." (1 Cor. 1:10-12)

The Christian church has been troubled by schism from the time of the New Testament. The churches of the sixteenth-century Reformation and especially those stemming from the Anabaptist reformers are no exception. The *Mennonite Encyclopedia* (Vol. V, p. xvi) lists seventeen denominations of Mennonites, Amish, and Brethren in Christ. In the history of the MC alone there have been at least twenty-five schisms.

In the past two decades, the MC and GCMC have been moving toward the goal of some form of unification by the end of the century. It remains to be seen whether the goal will be accomplished. Much depends on the seriousness and direction of the discernment process in the member congregations. Meanwhile, the leaders and members of the other Mennonite and BIC denominations look on with cautious curiosity.

The integration process received new impetus in a joint resolution adopted at Normal, Illinois, in 1989, when the two groups met together.

In relation to the matter of cooperation between the General Conference Mennonite Church and the Mennonite Church, we affirm the following:

1. We acknowledge that the Lord of the church is bringing us into close spiritual fellowship and increasing unity of faith and mission.

2. We believe that it is in the will of God to heal the part of our history which is a story of division and conflict. We also believe that God would be pleased to bring together that even larger part of our history which is the story of two different streams of the Mennonite family—the Dutch/North German/Russian and the Swiss/South German—who have come to North America and all persons who have become part of the Mennonite family.

3. We therefore commit ourselves to enter into a time of deliberate exploration of integration, until 1995, during which we will work at the following cooperative tasks and directions:

a. The articulation of a rationale for integration and the development of a common mission vision.

b. The undertaking in our congregations of a study of Christian unity.

c. The writing of a conjoint confession of faith.

d. The development of a leadership polity statement that would achieve a degree of unity sufficient for harmonious working relationships as a unified denomination.

e. The formation of a model, or models, of denominational structure at the area conference, national, and binational levels that would bring together the strengths of our current structures.

f. The continued movement toward integration of program activities and of area conference structures where the local situation makes it appropriate. In the case of program boards and agencies, we should pursue policies of program cooperation that move toward convergence but without the loss of separate denominational identities.

g. The deepening of mutual understanding through exchanges of personnel, fraternal visits, common publications, and the like.

4. We request that the current Committee on Cooperation conclude its work at Normal '89 and that a new conjoint committee be appointed by the General Boards to guide and implement the process outlined above, with regular reporting to the General Board and the biennial/triennial assemblies.

5. We propose that by 1995 we will discern whether or not to enter a period of actual integration of our two denominations based on the development of a complete plan for such integration. (Recommendation, 459)

Church Member Profile Findings

As a whole the respondents to the CMP I and II probes on church unity have favored the concept of cooperation (81%) more than the concept of integration or merger (16%). Between the two studies, the MCs gained a little support for integration (from 15% to 20%) while the GCs held steady at 26%.

On the question of whether or not to unite with some other Mennonite or Brethren in Christ group, the MC "yes" responses increased from 12% to 23% while the GC "yes" responses decreased from 24% to 22%. The affirmative responses in the MBC, BIC, and EMC groups were 14%, 10%, and 7%, respectively.

Over 40% of all groups are uncertain about integration, and among GCs the percentage uncertain actually increased from 43 to 48. Clearly much will depend on the discernment process in the congregations that is just beginning.

Among our four types of churches, liberal and transformist congregations favor church union more than conservative and separatist churches (28%, 25%, 19%, and 12%, respectively). The variation in attitudes is well illustrated in the following excerpts from our interviews with our representative members.

> *Sally Mae Stauffer, separatist-type church.* We're hearing a lot about integration, but I think we ought to hear more about the new divisions that might develop as a result. The resolution talks about reconciling our conflicts, but I believe our different cultural backgrounds have a lot more to do with it. We hear that Mennonites are limiting their witness in the world by being so fragmented, but there is more danger, it seems to me, of losing our influence as a small faithful separated people of God. Let's not be carried away by the "bigger is better" fallacy. The Lancaster Conference is large enough for me, and since there are so few GCs here we can't get very excited about the merger question.
>
> *Glenn Klassen, conservative-type church.* I've heard that some MCs and GCs oppose merger because they want to wait for the MBs, but I wouldn't count on that. I think an MC-GC merger could prod MBs to lead in getting the smaller groups together, especially among the so-called evangelical Mennonites. An MC-GC merger would create a large denomination that could become quite independent and they would have to work harder to develop good relationships with the smaller groups. For their part, MBs will certainly want to continue to cooperate with the MCs and GCs in programs like MCC.

Denise Preheim, liberal-type church. I'm very excited about the work of the Integration Committee. I hope it does not just listen to all the different points of view but plays an active advocacy role. I believe that integration is in keeping with Christ's prayer that his followers be united for the sake of effective witness in the world. By joining our ethnically separated conferences, we can discard some of our ethnocentric baggage that has obscured our message and together address the more important issues of discipleship.

Menno Isaac, transformist-type church: Being one of over seventy DCCs [dual conference churches], the members of our fellowship are much more alike than different. Although we came out of different conference churches, our covenant statement is the basis for a unity that transcends those differences.

Fortunately in Ontario we could join an area conference that was already a blend of the backgrounds we represent. The Mennonite Conference of Eastern Canada was a merger of three overlapping conferences—one MC, one GC, and one Amish Mennonite (MC). After years of living in the same towns and cities and doing many things together, the groups finally merged in 1988 as the first truly inter-Mennonite area conference.

It may not be as simple a process to get our other conferences together, but I am confident the end result would be worth the time and energy it would take. I believe integration would strengthen, not weaken, our outreach and our peace witness as we work together on these things and help each other stand up for love and peace in the arenas of domestic and international conflict and injustice.

The MCs have had the best record on conscientious objection to military service and the GCs have had the best witness on the nonpayment of taxes used for military purposes. By getting our acts together, we would tell the world that Mennonites not only withdraw into CO camps but also witness to the nations against the evils of war.

In light of conflicting emotions on this issue, the MC/GC Integration Exploration Committee is aware that strong cases can be made for a continuation of the present pattern of independent bodies working together as well as for a more intentional integration or merger of existing bodies. Committee members also know that if the churches are to move toward integration, a strong rationale will be needed. In providing motivation, the committee is determined to appeal to the highest thinking of their people rather than the more self-centered motive, "What will we get out of this?"

Three Models for Church Unity

In its work so far, the committee has developed two main models for church unity, with a third model also being suggested.

1. *The Cooperation Mode*. Under this model, the two denominations would continue to exist while conjoint programs of mission and service would be further developed. Their number and range are already im-

pressive (see P. Kraybill, 445-9). Cooperation permits members to express unity through fellowship and working together, all the while respecting different cultural roots and identities. Cooperation motivates increased responsibility at local levels.

Cooperation enables members to maintain and cultivate relationships with other Anabaptist-Mennonite groups. It allows them to work at mutual ministries without investing time and energy in structural unity. "Mennonite Central Committee illustrates the beauty of respecting the diversity of its supporting groups while working cooperatively with a heart for common mission" (IEC, 10).

The cooperation model is nothing new; it has been underway for much of the twentieth century. Cooperation is what we have now. Vern Preheim, GC general secretary, has commented that

> at a certain point, more cooperation ceases to make sense because only a complete integration makes sense. Some believe that MC and GCMC have reached the level of cooperation where we need to move expeditiously to integration or else pull back on cooperation, especially with regard to the number of dual conference congregations.

2. *The Integration Mode.* This model calls for unification of the two groups into one. It calls for new identity and structures, common goals, a new sense of interdependence and division of roles, and a new system of accountability. The shape of the organization that would be needed has yet to be discerned, but the committee has listed a number of compelling reasons to bring the MC/GC integration process to full realization.

> 1. *To witness more effectively for Jesus Christ to a world in need of reconciliation.* It was the special prayer of Christ "that they may be one . . . so that the world may believe that you have sent me" (John 17:23). While the continued separation of believers needs to be rationalized, integration needs no rationale. It should be enough to remember that Jesus wills it. The visible expression of love and unity makes the gospel credible to the world. Organizational unity is not the heart of Christian unity, but it does communicate our covenant with each other and therefore strengthens our witness. Sharing our programs and financial resources will make possible a greater mission effort to a world of need.
>
> 2. *To confess our common faith heritage as Mennonite Church and General Conference Mennonite Church bodies.* Our history is a patchwork of different cultures and life journeys set against the background of a common faith origin. The heritage of our shared beginnings has drawn us to a convergence of beliefs and practices. Integration will strengthen the Anabaptist-Mennonite vision of faith and practice.
>
> 3. *To present a stronger voice for the Anabaptist-Mennonite vision in the larger Christian community.* Believers of other traditions are urging Mennonites to share our biblical insights and practical learnings from generations of believers church history. In our fragmentation we Mennonites have limited

our visibility to other Christians. Integration would provide greater visibility and larger resources for faith conversation with other believers.

4. *To promote a process of unity already initiated by the leading of the Holy Spirit.* Significant development of inter-Mennonite cooperation since World War I, such as alternative service projects and Mennonite Central Committee, has moved us toward each other in ways unprecedented at any time in our history. Our two denominations have worked together in joint statements of faith and in joint programs of education, service, and church development. Numerous dually-affiliated congregations and one dually-related district conference have already chosen to live as one people of God. Integration would permit this process of unity to come to fuller expression.

5. *To strengthen the life of the church by creating unified and expanded program structures.* Consolidation of resources both spiritual and financial would create a broader base from which to minister, allowing for new programs to be created and existing ones to be improved or expanded. Duplication of organization would be eliminated, freeing both personnel and funds for further use in God's kingdom. Integration would offer structures that better serve the mission of the church.

6. *To simplify the relationships of our African American, Latino and other newer people groups to each other and to the larger church.* Both of our denominations have worked among the same ethnic groups. Believers from these groups find importance in fellowship and work with their own people across denominational lines. They do not find denominational differences to be important. Integration would strengthen the life and work of these groups.

7. *To affirm that God has a larger future purpose that calls us to be a more faithful people.* God has bestowed numerous blessings upon us in the past, albeit as two separate denominational groups. However, the past does not necessarily represent the best that God has for us in the future. There is an unfolding picture of what can be that should motivate us towards unity. Integration would cause us to reexamine Christ's vision for the church and allow us to realize that vision more fully. (IEC, 470)

One reason some committee members are wary about the integration model is the risk of pushing too hard and losing everything. If too much reaction sets in, the whole question could be tabled indefinitely. They do not want to give the impression that premature decisions are being made by an elite committee. Therefore, a third model is being suggested that advocates gradual rather than total integration of structures, allowing for acceptable overlap and duplication.

3. *The Decentralized Unity Mode.* This is the cooperation mode with a significant difference. At some point in 1995 or toward the end of this century, the two bodies would adopt a new resolution declaring as of that date that they are henceforth one denomination with a new identity—the United (or Uniting) Mennonite Church. While no new structures would need to be an immediate part of the resolution, the declaration itself would be a powerful stimulus for accelerated, progressive

integration of structures, just as the decision to create one MC/GC seminary in Indiana led to further inevitable integration over time.

No doubt the mission boards would begin to consult about common concerns of mission principle and strategy and gradually spend more time together processing common agenda. The editors of the respective church papers would share more articles and editorials and eventually merge publications. No one would have to worry about how long it would take or whether to integrate all structures, because the church would already be united in principle.

An image for the third model was suggested by Robert L. Ramseyer, GC missionary to Japan and former missions professor.

> It used to be assumed that the ideal marriage was one in which two people somehow merged themselves, gave up their separate identities, and formed one new joint personality, each forming half of that new personality. We now know that a good marriage does not mean that we give up our individual identities, but rather in our commitment to working together we develop richer and fuller individual identities. . . .
>
> As the leaders of the General Conference Mennonite Church and the Mennonite Church explore the issue of unity among us, let them look once more at the marriage and AMBS models of working together. Just as two people in marriage bring separate identities which need to be allowed to develop and grow rather than to be given up in a marriage merger, so too do the GCMC and MC have separate, different, and valuable identities. . . . These are not differences which necessarily conflict. They can enrich and stimulate us as we work together. Before the momentum toward merger/integration overwhelms us, we need to ask whether giving up these identities is really what God is asking of us. Can we not work closely together in Christian unity without being [totally] merged/integrated into a new identity formed by giving up valuable but different ideas about what it means to be a disciple and a church in today's world? (Ramseyer, 379)

Summary and Conclusion

In this chapter we examined changes affecting the historical profiles of the five denominations participating in the Church Member Profile research project. We took special note of the differences between them and of the fact that in our earlier study we had failed to give sufficient weight to the diversity within the so-called Anabaptist-Mennonite family of churches.

We found Rodney Sawatsky's recent chapter on the recovery of Mennonite pluralism especially helpful as a method of classifying Mennonite and Brethren in Christ congregations into four types, renamed separatist, conservative, liberal, and transformist. In the rest of our book, these will be the four main types of congregational environment for the discernment of important moral, ethical, and otherwise spiritual issues.

We began the discernment process by looking at the question of church unity. We discovered that separatist churches are the least interested in church unity as measured by our CMP probes, followed by the conservative, transformist, and liberal churches, in that order. We also discovered that in all four types, between 40 and 50% of the members are uncertain whether their denomination should become integrated with another Mennonite or Brethren in Christ group. The members as a whole appear to be undecided and open to further exploration of this question.

Then we looked at three models of unity and discovered that 81% of all groups favored the cooperation model and 16% the integration or merger model. We looked at the definitions of those models given by the MC/GC Integration Exploration Committee and ended with a third option, called the decentralized unity mode. This solution would permit the integration of denominations without the immediate sacrifice of individual identities.

At the end of his chapter, Sawatsky raised a crucial question for our study of the discerning, although divergent, people of God. "Can a perspective be both pluralistic and normative?" (Sawatsky, 151). His question implied that the recognition of four types of churches, each having its own interpretation of theological and ethical issues, complicates the search for norms by which the discernment process can move toward consensus.

While affirming both pluralism and normativeness, Sawatsky made no new attempt to redefine the Anabaptist vision to embrace the variant directions the movement took then and is taking now, except for one concluding admonition: "Live for the one while embracing the many!" (Sawatsky, 152). That is what we will attempt to do in the rest of this book.

Discussion Questions

1. In view of the catch phrases used in this chapter to characterize each of the five denominations, what can we learn from each other about what it means to be faithful Christians?

2. How do you explain the inverse relationship between the percentage of members recruited from outside (the evangelistic norm) and the percentage of members adhering to pacifism (the nonresistance norm)? Is it possible to preach the gospel of salvation and the gospel of peace at the same time?

3. What are the strengths and weaknesses of each of the four types of churches—separatist, conservative, liberal, and transformist?

4. Which of the following best expresses your opinion about coopera-

tion between the various Mennonite and Brethren in Christ denominations?

a. There should be fewer cooperative activities than there are now.

b. Cooperation should be maintained about at current levels.

c. Cooperative activities and programs should be gradually increased as specific needs arise.

d. Every effort should be made toward eventual integration of as many programs and institutions as possible. Tabulate your answers on the chalkboard and discuss.

CHAPTER 3

Discernment in the Church as the Body of Christ

Now you are the body of Christ and individually members of it.
—1 Corinthians 12:27

IN ALL FIVE DENOMINATIONS that participated in the Church Member Profile research project, it is hoped that each congregation is a vital part of Christ's worldwide church. Christ has called the members of each congregation to be his body in its own location (John 20:21, 1 Cor. 12:27).

Nevertheless, there is considerable variation of attitudes among the congregations as to what it means to be the body of Christ. Many members have a rather limited view of the role of the local congregation in the plan of Christ according to the Scriptures. They know themselves to be sinners in constant need of God's grace, and they view the church as a sanctuary where impotent Christians go to receive the means of grace through worship and communion, hymns and prayers, preaching and teaching. This image of the church as a passive group of frail members needs challenge.

Responses to the Church Member Profile questionnaire indicate that members of the five denominations overwhelmingly (99%) affirm both Jesus' humanity and divinity. Almost the only difference between the four types of church was whether or not doubts are expressed concerning the *meaning* of affirming both the humanity and divinity of Jesus. Slightly more members of integrationist-type churches (conservative and liberal) express some doubts (14% and 20%, respectively) while more members of separationist-type churches (separatist and transformist) say they have no doubts (95% and 88%, respectively).

We also note that in churches of every type, Jesus is seen more "as the personal Savior who died for our sins" than as "the suffering servant who calls us to follow his example." However, 39% of the members of liberal-type churches prefer the suffering servant identity of Jesus, in contrast to 20% for the conservative churches. It might seem that these same liberal-type churches which affirm the suffering servant role for Jesus would also affirm it for his followers, but that is not the case. The percentage of those who agree that Christian believers who truly follow Christ in all of life can expect to face criticism from and persecution by the larger society is lowest for the liberal churches (59% compared to 72% for the separatist churches). Obviously, many members maintain a wide separation between Christ's role and ours. Denise Preheim expressed her doubts.

> I'm not always sure what it means to follow Christ in all of life. I read the Bible to try to find out who Christ is, how he interacted with humans, and what he expects of me in response. I haven't quite figured out what his divinity is all about. When you're a child, you talk about heaven, and when you grow up you're less sure where heaven is. I have kind of a metaphysical idea about what it is, and I believe Christ was speaking to that quite directly. I hope to sort it out a lot more by rereading the Gospels. I certainly see the Gospels as more authoritative on this subject than the epistles, and I look to the Gospels for an understanding of who Christ was, what his relationship to God was, and what his relationship is to me.

But what was Christ's vision for his church? At a study conference on Christology (held in Normal, Illinois, August 4-6, 1989 and attended by representatives from four of the five CMP II denominations), two contrasting views of the church were presented concerning the person and work of Christ. George Brunk III spoke on "The Exclusiveness of Jesus Christ." Brunk referred to "the tension between the finality of Christ and the finitude of the church," and rejected easing that tension as we carry the burden "to represent [Christ's] exclusiveness through the actions and structures of finite history and imperfect humanity." Thus we must always, at least in theory, "make a clear distinction between the finality of Christ and the human condition of the church in all of its aspects," for in the last analysis, "the exclusiveness of Jesus Christ *is not transmitted* to his followers" (Brunk III, A, 26, italics added).

In the other paper, MB theologian John E. Toews spoke of Jesus Christ as "The Convener of the Church." Toews chose this strange, fresh title to assert (on the basis of a convincing review of the relevant New Testament texts) that Jesus' mission as the Christ was indeed *transmitted to his followers* (John 20:21), and that "Jesus builds the church as a kingdom outpost of ethical discernment." Toews added that "the church is the gathered people of God discerning what it means to live as the people of God in the world, and to hold each other accountable to the consensus discerned" (J. Toews, 10).

Brunk and Toews wrote their papers independently of each other on different assigned topics; their theses are not as far apart as it seems. At the end of this chapter, we will return to the dialogue between them implicit in their papers.

The Mandate to Bind and Loose

What does it mean to be the gathered people of God, discerning what to believe and how to live as God's people in the world? In the remainder of this chapter we will examine several New Testament texts (then continue the quest from somewhat different vantage points in the two chapters that follow). We begin with Matthew 16:17-19, the great divide in the public ministry of Jesus between the months of preparation and the final weeks of culmination.

> Blessed are you, Simon son of Jonah! For flesh and blood has not revealed this to you, but my Father in heaven. And I tell you, you are Peter, and on this rock I will build my church, and the gates of Hades will not prevail against it. I will give you the keys of the kingdom of heaven, and whatever you bind on earth will be bound in heaven, and whatever you loose on earth will be loosed in heaven.

Until this moment, Jesus had preached and taught much about the gospel of the kingdom of heaven, inviting the people to repent and believe the gospel (Mark 1:14-15; Matt. 4:23). His preaching was primarily proclaiming the gospel to persons at the point of their *unbelief*, and his teaching was unfolding that gospel to persons at the point of their *belief*.

The first sign of Jesus' intention to establish a church was his calling of twelve persons to follow him (Mark 3:13-19, Matt. 10:2-4), to form a company to share his mission, to become a new prototype of the old covenanted people of God, and to be trained to continue his mission after his departure.

At a point near Caesarea Philippi when it appeared that his mission had reached a crucial juncture, Jesus asked the disciples this pair of questions: "Who do people say that I am? Who do you say that I am?" Peter's reply, "You are the Christ, the Son of the living God," occasioned Jesus' first mention of building his church on the rock of Peter's charter confession of faith.

The word church (*ekklesia*) was used 109 times in the New Testament but only three times in the Gospels—and there only in Matthew in two texts, of which this is the first. Both texts contain Christ's mandate to his church to bind and loose, or as the Living Bible puts it, to lock some doors and open others. Moreover, that mandate defines the church. The church is where Jesus is confessed as the Christ and believers are enjoined to bind and loose each other in the perspective of the kingdom of heaven. The church is the gathering of Christ's people in a meeting for worship and discernment.

The imagery of binding and loosing refers to four intended functions for the church. In the most literal sense, it means to engage in moral-ethical discernment of what is right and wrong, assessing what behavior should be encouraged and what behavior should be discouraged. When questions about the law of Moses and some particular application came before the rabbis of Jesus' time, they made binding and loosing rulings. If a certain adherence was required, the people were "bound" to it; if not, they were "loosed" from it. Thus the mandate implies not only intellectual discernment but also decision making about truth and error in our thinking as well as rightness and wrongness in our behavior.

In a broader sense, to bind and loose means deliberating on related matters affecting the believer's faith and life, such as the conditions of entry into the church, the continuing response to the lordship of Christ, the formation of an appropriate spirituality and lifestyle for believers, and the discernment of gifts for the assignment of roles in the work of the church. Even among the rabbis, the discussion soon shifted from behavioral rules to behavioral principles. Rabbinic decisions over time were formulated and disseminated in a form called *halachah*—principles which could be confirmed or revised from one generation to another as times changed and new insights emerged (Epstein, 512).

More specifically, the verbs refer to the binding and loosing of Satan (Matt. 12:29; Mark 3:27; Rev. 20: 2, 7) and the loosing of persons bound by Satan (Luke 13:16). The image of the "gates of Hades" refers to the domain and influence of Satan. The church is taught to take the reality of Satan seriously. Satan is a personal influence in the lives of persons (Mark 1:12-13), resulting in harmful behavior of many kinds. Satan is also the impersonal powers and principalities of this present darkness (Eph. 6:12), resulting in what has been called systemic evil in society, in which Christians too often participate knowingly or unknowingly (Henderson, 191-205).

By ignoring in its preaching, teaching, and group process the personal and systemic reality of a demonic power in the universe, the church unwittingly reinforces demonic influence, for sin is like "a little yeast [that] leavens the whole batch of dough" (1 Cor. 5:6). The disciples knew what binding and loosing meant to the rabbis, but they were probably shocked to hear Jesus giving them and the future church the authority to bind Satan and to loose persons from his perverse influence.

The Church Member Profile reveals that 98% of the members of the five denominations believe that "Satan, as a personal devil, is active in the world today"—90% definitely, 5% probably, and 3% possibly; but it is still a shock to many to hear that our congregations are authorized by Christ to bind and loose in relation to this belief. There was some hedging on this question by members of the liberal churches, only 75% of whom said "definitely," but even there affirmation of a personal devil is evident.

Still more specifically, binding and loosing refers to forgiveness and retention of sins. This dimension is explicit in the John 20:23 parallel to binding and loosing. "If you forgive the sins of any, they are forgiven; if you retain the sins of any, they are retained." The centrality of forgiveness in the teaching of Jesus is seen in numerous texts. We are to forgive so that we ourselves can be forgiven (Matt. 6:12-15). We are to forgive so people can be healed (Mark 2:5). We are to forgive not just seven times but seventy times seven, as often as the person repents and seeks restoration (Matt. 18:21-22).

The binding and loosing functions examined so far are not unrelated. There are three ways in which the two functions of discernment and forgiveness are interrelated (Yoder, B, 5-7). First, *forgiveness assumes prior discernment*. Unless there is prior consensus in the congregation as to what is right or wrong, it is impossible to bind and loose. To "forgive the sins of any" or to "retain the sins of any" (John 20:23), the church must first clarify and specify the moral-ethical standards by which sin is defined.

Second, *forgiveness facilitates discernment*. If faulty standards are used to reprove a brother or sister, the best way to show this is by face-to-face conversation aimed at reconciliation. By this procedure, the group's standards are tested and changed if they lack foundation.

Third, *forgiveness helps people accept differences*. As we gain practice in the giving and receiving of admonitions in the church, we quickly become aware that many amoral matters should be left to personal variations in preference and lifestyle.

> If Christians have been accustomed to dealing with one another in love and finding that they are able to be reconciled whenever they deal with a matter [of alleged offense] in love, they find as well that their "tolerance threshold" rises—i.e., a spirit of mutual trust arises in which fewer "differences" offend. (Yoder, B, 6)

Discernment and the Rule of Christ

We turn next to the text in Matthew 18:15-20.

> If another member of the church sins against you, go and point out the fault when the two of you are alone. If the member listens to you, you have

regained that one. But if you are not listened to, take one or two others along with you, so that every word may be confirmed by the evidence of two or three witnesses. If the member refuses to listen to them, tell it to the church; and if the offender refuses to listen even to the church, let such a one be to you as a Gentile and a tax collector.

Truly I tell you, whatever you bind on earth will be bound in heaven, and whatever you loose on earth will be loosed in heaven. Again, truly I tell you, if two of you agree on earth about anything you ask, it will be done for you by my Father in heaven. For where two or three are gathered in my name, I am there among them.

Here the context for binding and loosing is not the confession of Peter but a series of teachings of Jesus about such things as true greatness in the kingdom of heaven, temptations to sin, the parable of the lost sheep, the parable of the unforgiving servant, and the teaching on loving correction and reconciliation.

The second person pronouns in the first paragraph are all in the singular "you," but in the second paragraph they are in the plural "you." As Yoder explains, "This suggests that the authorization [of the second paragraph] may have a broader import for the church than that of the immediate disciplinary context [of the first paragraph]" (Yoder, B, 5).

Moreover, the first paragraph has to do with sinful behavior of all kinds, not limited to interpersonal offenses. The phrase "against you" in some versions is not found in the best manuscripts or in Luke 17:3 and is omitted in the Jerusalem Bible and the New English Bible. They read simply, "If your brother [or sister] does something wrong. . ." or "If your brother [or sister] commits a sin. . . ." The teaching is less about how to deal with the specific offense of one member against another than about how to deal with the sins of all church members in general.

In other words, this is more of a positive "Rule of Christ," as the Anabaptists called it, for overcoming the sinful tendencies of all of us in the church than it is a negative procedure for discipline of a particular member. Certainly the objective is not to expel anyone but to facilitate reconciliation and renewal in the church. The Anabaptist leader Conrad Grebel caught this meaning when he advised Thomas Muentzer to "march forward with the Word and create a Christian church with the help of Christ and his rule as we find it instituted in Matthew 18 and practiced in the epistles" (L. Harder, C, 289).

This Rule of Christ is meant for every member, not just for the person sinned against or for the leadership of the church. It is a model that Jesus gave for the reconciling discernment process in his church.

1. The process is a conversation between persons who differ, one of whom takes the responsibility to initiate the conversation.

2. They enter into the conversation because they truly seek the reconciliation of their differences.

3. Their conflict broadens gradually to include others needed to achieve reconciliation.

4. The effectiveness of the reconciliation procedure is enhanced by hearing knowledgeable witnesses who confirm the rightness or wrongness of the allegations.

5. The deliberation is surrounded by the congregation, which ultimately will ratify either the reconciliation or the impossibility of reconciliation.

6. Although the goal is reconciliation, not exclusion, the congregation forthrightly acknowledges the situation in which a recalcitrant party to the conversation refuses to be reconciled.

7. The discernment reached by this process stands ratified in heaven. (Yoder, J, 27)

The Matthew 18 "binding and loosing" text appears even more sweeping than its parallel Matthew 16 text. Not only is the phrase repeated, "whatever you bind on earth will be bound in heaven," heaven is also committed to whatever two or three agree about in Christ's name. This surely does not mean that two or three are always right in whatever they agree in Christ's name. Rather, when they begin their conversation with an open and redemptive review of their differences and come to a point of reconciliation, their consensus will be ratified in heaven.

Discernment and the Help of the Holy Spirit

Jesus promised that he would somehow be in the midst of his people whenever they gathered in his name (Matt. 18:20). In the Gospel of John, the gift of the Holy Spirit following Christ's resurrection precedes the discernment mandate (John 20:22-23). The prospect of the ongoing presence of the risen Lord and the empowerment of the Holy Spirit are part of the same promise undergirding the church in its binding and loosing, forgiving, witnessing, and discerning ministries. The connection between the ascent of Christ and the descent of the Holy Spirit is indicated in the following passage from John 16:7-8, 12-14.

> It is to your advantage that I go away, for if I do not go away, the Advocate will not come to you; but if I go, I will send him to you. And when he comes, he will prove the world wrong about sin and righteousness and judgment. . . . I still have many things to say, but you cannot bear them now. When the Spirit of truth comes, he will guide you into all the truth; for he will not speak on his own, but will speak whatever he hears, and he will declare to you the things that are to come. He will glorify me, because he will take what is mine and declare it to you.

The Greek noun variously translated *Advocate* (NRSV, NEB, Jerusalem Bible), *Counselor* (RSV, NIV), and *Helper* (TEV, Phillips), comes from the Greek *parakletos,* the basic meaning of which is someone to abide with you, to aid and guide you, to be your instructor and support. The term was applied both to Jesus Christ (1 John 2:1) and to the Holy Spirit, who is "another Paraclete" (John 14:16). The Paraclete is continuous with Jesus Christ but not to be simply identified as the same person. He is the "alter ego of Jesus" (Howard, 727). He is the invisible, risen, abiding Spirit of Jesus in the midst of his gathered people, constantly bringing to the church's remembrance all that Jesus taught and did during his earthly ministry (John 14:26).

The use of the personal pronoun indicates that the Paraclete is fully human and divine, just as Jesus was both human and divine. The Paraclete's function is preeminently to guide the members of the church in their ongoing discernment of the ways of the heavenly kingdom, with testimony, admonition, advocacy, prophecy, forgiveness, and empowerment being the functions of that mandate.

The Paraclete is the Spirit of truth (John 14:17; 15:26; 16:13), who will confirm and clarify the teachings of Jesus, "interpreting them to the church according to the contemporary need . . . under fresh conditions" (Howard, 712-3). Taking the place of the physical presence of Jesus, the Paraclete will abide with his followers in their continuing mission in the world.

The Paraclete will empower church members for their renewed counterattacks on the "ruler of this world" (John 16:8-11), reveal the mind of Christ more fully than could be known by the first disciples (John 16:11-13), and enable disciples of every generation to fulfill their discipleship (John 15:26-27). It will be to their advantage that Jesus depart and send the Paraclete, for then they will discern the truth for themselves in fulfillment of all that Jesus has begun to teach them. This discernment will concern not only past and present realities but also "the things that are to come" (John 16:13).

Summary and Conclusion

As members of 2,020 congregations under study in the CMP II research project, our response to the grandeur of Christ's intention to build his church with believers like Peter, the fisherman, is surely one of shock, as it undoubtedly was for Peter and the other disciples. It is amazing to read that Jesus gave his church the keys to the kingdom of heaven and commissioned his church to bind and loose on earth things that will then be bound and loosed in heaven.

The surprise is magnified when we read about Christ's rule for overcoming the sinful inclinations of all of us in the church. Glenn Klassen wasn't sure that the church today still believes in this rule of Christ and whether it could apply to his problem with the neighbor who plugged his tiles.

Our mental and emotional sensibilities are further shaken by the story of Christ's ascendance from the earth and his replacement on earth by his alter ego, the Advocate, the Spirit of truth, whose role is to abide with all congregations, helping members to become the discerning people of God.

Certainly George Brunk III was not entirely wrong when he said that the exclusiveness of Jesus Christ is not transmittable to his followers. But then what are we to do with John 20:21 (RSV), "As the Father has sent me, even so I send you"?

John E. Toews was talking about Christ's vision for the church, not about the failure of the church to live up to that vision. He ends on this note:

> The challenge facing Mennonite churches is to recover and expand our historic theology of the church as an authentic discipling and disciplining community. That recovery and reshaping will require a genuine spiritual renewal and empowerment because all the forces of our culture move us away from such a theology and sociology. (J. Toews, 24)

Brunk acknowledged that although the exclusiveness of Christ is not transmittable to us, neither can we as church members disassociate ourselves from it.

> The church as a new community is to demonstrate the more-than-they level of righteousness (Matt. 5) that is made possible because of the empowerment of Christ's final salvation. . . . In a derivative sense, therefore, the church participates in Christ's finality. . . . This role will never become easy . . . but woe to us if the burden is not carried. (Brunk III, A, 26-7)

Brunk and Toews are both right. The seeming contradiction of their theses is in reality a single truth standing on its head to gain attention. The thesis of the one is contained in that of the other as time is contained in eternity—the life of eternity that has already begun here on earth. Christ is exclusive, but he calls us to be the discerning body of Christ, distinguishing truth from error, binding each other to righteous behavior and loosing each other from unrighteous behavior, binding Satan and loosing persons bound by Satan's rule in the world, opening doors of truth and closing doors of untruth, and forgiving and retaining the sins of each other.

We hope that as we work our way through the chapters of this study book, we will grasp more of what it can mean to become the discerning people of God.

Discussion Questions

1. What do you think Jesus meant by instructing his disciples to bind and loose? Has binding and loosing been part of your experience as a Christian? Is it really possible to make binding and loosing moral-ethical decisions? To bind Satan?

2. Can you feel in unity with a brother or sister in the church while disagreeing on moral-ethical questions?

3. What has been your experience of the practice of church discipline in the church? If mostly negative, does it help to read that the Rule of Christ was meant as a positive, healing ministry in which we all participate as recipients as well as initiators of a forgiving ministry? Is the Matthew 18 Rule of Christ practiced in your congregation?

4. What should the church do with members who refuse to be reconciled with each other and with the teachings of the church?

CHAPTER 4

Discernment in the Church as a Biblical Community

Then beginning with Moses and all the prophets,
he interpreted to them the things . . . in all the scriptures.
—Luke 24:27

THE BIBLE IS THE SOURCE BOOK for the discerning people of God. Without the Bible we would grope in darkness for a normative guide for our faith and ethics. Christ is our authority, but the Bible is the only place where we meet the historical Jesus. The Holy Spirit is our guide, but the Bible is the connecting link between the Spirit's work and the Lord of the church. The Bible contains the means for testing whether the member's witness to having been so guided is continuous with what Jesus did and taught. God is our source of truth, but we need the framework of the Bible to gauge whether or not the word that is heard in the congregation is truly God's word.

It is in the Scriptures of the Old and New Testaments that the people of God find a reliable guide for belief and discipleship. By affirming the Bible as our trustworthy guide for righteous living, we dare believe that in Scripture we will find answers to our deepest questions about life and death, sin and salvation, prejudice and suffering, truth and error, moral and immoral behavior.

Affirmations like this often refer to the private reading of the Bible for personal guidance—but the Bible is preeminently the church's book. This is evident whenever the Bible is read to the people at public worship, but it should also be read for congregational discussion and discernment. We might even say that to read the Bible in the fellowship of the church is what creates the church in each generation (Matt.16:18-19).

The members of the participant CMP II churches certainly believe in the Bible's authority. Ninety-four percent believe either that the Bible is

55

"the divinely inspired and inerrant Word of God, the only trustworthy guide for faith and life" (78%) or "the authoritative Word of God and a reliable guide, but not inerrant" (16%). Separatists are most inclined (91%) and liberals least inclined (61%) to accept biblical inerrancy. Nevertheless, the vast majority of the members of all four church types affirm the Bible as God's Word.

When asked, however, how often they studied the Bible, "seeking to understand it and letting it speak to you," one-fifth of the conservative as well as liberal churches answered "seldom" or "never." Another one-fourth could answer only "occasionally." Comments by our four representative members help us to understand these percentages.

Sally Mae Stauffer, separatist. I believe God can reveal himself to me through my daily reading the Word, but I'm not sure how or when that happens. I don't quite understand it, but then I don't understand a lot of things that happen. We just go on living, trusting our minister to preach the true Word of God to us.

Glenn Klassen, conservative. As my life unfolds, I'm really looking forward to doing more devotional and group Bible study, but I'm not sure my church has an adequate program for this apart from the traditional Sunday school class. In Sunday school we use the Mennonite Brethren quarterly. It isn't every Sunday that I get a big blessing out of it, but occasionally something new comes out. It's usually something the teacher says. In our class he does most of the talking, although last Sunday we really got into a discussion when we started talking about whether or not to build a new church. Someone asked what our intentions would be in building a new church. Was it just because we have an edifice complex, or was it to be a reaching out with the Word of God? Would we work harder at evangelism if we had a new church? At the end of the hour there was no real yes or no, but only opinions expressed—really nothing very significant.

One of these months we'll make the decision by majority vote without any clear Holy Spirit consensus. We've never really experienced a time of Bible study that was a breakthrough on anything. It takes discipline, and sometimes I'm really hungry for it, which sounds corny when I say it like that; but when you haven't done it for awhile and you go back to it, it really feels good to get scripturally squared away again.

Denise Preheim, liberal. Before the General Conference sessions in Saskatoon in 1986, our church had five Sunday evening meetings in a row about human sexuality and talking about different aspects of it—premarital sex, teenage sex, extramarital sex, homosexuality. Throughout the whole thing, there was no clear discernment, no statement adopted to take to Saskatoon. Very little Scripture was brought into it, no resolution saying that according to the Bible premarital sex is wrong, extramarital sex is wrong, homosexuality is wrong.

Homosexuality is a tough issue no one wants to touch because there's a gay person in our church who gets all offended if anyone even questions whether or not homosexuality might not be right. I certainly don't have the answer on that question and I'm not sure you can take that one to the Bible for light. I believe the Bible is a guide for our lives, but there's a lot of times when people see things differently and come to a different understanding of what something says. I think people on both sides of an issue can find Scripture proof texts for their opinions.

Menno Isaac, transformist. When we study the Bible in our Fellowship, I get two contrasting feelings. One is that I'm in another world remote from my life and work at Honeywell. The Bible knows nothing about computer chips, and Honeywell knows nothing about the kingdom of God. But the other feeling is that the Bible knows an awful lot about Honeywell, and I get vibes all the time about what's right and wrong there.

Certainly much of my work at Honeywell is done in the framework of the creative power of God that we read about in Genesis 1 and particularly God's mandate to us to use and subdue the resources he has created. And then I read in that same Bible about the human tendency to become autonomous creators ourselves to the point where we no longer acknowledge God's purposes, for we put ourselves into God's place—the ultimate idolatry.

The major theme I see in the Bible from old covenant to new is God's progressive revelation to us, supremely in Jesus Christ, seeking to free us from the self-deception of our ultimate idolatry and to enlist us as his people in that mission. Over and over again I marvel at the clarity of the Bible in spelling out God's mission and ours in relation to such biblical themes as creation, vocation, judgment, redemption, covenant, and discipleship.

And over and over again I get renewed in my desire, with the help and support of my brothers and sisters in the Fellowship, to seek first God's kingdom and to let the computer chips fall where they will. I see the church and the Bible as interdependent. The Bible apart from the church becomes an object of idolatry, and the church apart from the Bible soon loses its saltiness and can't be distinguished from other human institutions like Honeywell.

The Concept of the Biblical Community

In one sense we're talking about the Christian education of adults. Seventy-one percent of the members of the five denominations attend Sunday school all or most Sundays. This varies from 82% in the separatist churches to 58% in the liberal churches. If these classes were conducted as serious fellowships in which the Bible was read and discussed as the "trustworthy guide for faith and life," the members would constantly experience what it means to be the discerning people of God.

In a deeper sense we're talking about changing our idea of the local congregation along the lines of the discernment mandate discussed in the previous chapter. In his book, *The Bible in Human Transformation: A New Paradigm for Biblical Study*, Walter Wink declares that most Bible study in the Sunday school today is bankrupt because it no longer serves the function for which the Scriptures were intended: to call forth and increase faith and faithfulness.

Bible study has been primarily intellectual, separating "theory from

practice, mind from body, reason from emotion, knowledge from experience." Moreover, Bible study has been separated from a vital Christian
community, to the detriment of our capacity "to deal with the real problems of actual living persons in their daily lives" (Wink, A, 6, 10-11).

Wink believes Bible study for human transformation should be done
in community, primarily in small groups of twenty or fewer persons, so
everyone can be actively involved. He describes some of his experiences
with Bible study groups.

> I have seen people discover together insights not one of them knew before
> entering the room. I have watched them meld into what I can only describe
> as a corporate brain, one person saying one thing and another building on
> it, and another on that, until together they have produced ideas they would
> never alone in all their lives have been able to think their way to—and
> which no exegete had previously discovered. When otherwise undistin-
> guished people discover such unimaginable capacities in themselves and
> one another, the discovery is unhinging. They are not soon satisfied with
> any other approach. (Wink, B, 67-68)

In several respects the possibilities of the biblical congregation go beyond Wink's group model. His groups seem to move in only one direction—from the biblical text to its application in the lives of the participants. Despite his references to a "corporate brain," he leaves application
to the personal responsibility of each member and rejects the goal of consensus in the group and the function of binding and loosing discussed in
our previous chapter.

In Willard Swartley's book *Slavery, Sabbath, War, and Women: Case Issues in Biblical Interpretation* we find a more complete view of the biblical
community. First of all, we discover that we can also move in the other
direction—from our contemporary moral-ethical issues back to the "ethical heart of the Bible" for guidance. We learn that the Bible can be used to
address the social-ethical issues that we bring to it, like the four illustra-
tions in the book of slavery, sabbath, war, and women.

"As one grasps the central ethical imperative of the total Bible and
then looks at these case issues and others from this vantage point, differences in interpretation may be resolved and consensus may emerge. Jesus' own example in transcending scribal arguments over which law is
greatest instructs us here. By appealing to the ethical heart of the entire
law (Deut. 6:4 and Lev. 19:18), Jesus taught that all moral obligation is
based on love for God and love for the neighbor. . . . By giving priority to
this moral imperative of love, we may be able to achieve consensus on
the four issues of this study" (Swartley, 203-4).

Swartley goes on to say

- that the Bible is not just one resource among many but "the essential source" for ethical discernment and decision making,
- that the "community of faith is the proper context in which Scripture is to be understood,"
- that "only within communities of faith should one expect to find the variety of gifts essential to perceive fully and interpret adequately the biblical teachings,
- that "only within such communities should one expect to find the spiritual resources essential to the motivation and empowerment for living as the biblical teachings envision,"
- that "the discerning community of believers plays an important role in validating interpretation,"
- that "God's Spirit plays a creative, illuminative role in biblical interpretation,"
- that each of us is to test our interpretation of Scripture "with brothers and sisters in the believing community,"
- and that "the insights and truth claims of one community should be shared with and tested by other communities of faith." (Swartley, 210, 215, 217, 223, 337, 234)

The Principle of Alternation

If deliberation in the Christian fellowship of brothers and sisters searching the Scriptures together is the proper means of spiritual-ethical discernment, members need always to be open to change when the truth comes. Peter Berger calls this *the experience of alternation,* opening oneself to the possibility that the alternative to what one presently believes is true may in fact be true (Berger, A, 10, 17ff.). This idea gives us another tension in the discernment process—on one hand "to contend for the faith that was once for all entrusted to the saints" (Jude 3) and on the other hand to remain always open to the possibility that certain aspects of the way we view the faith may need minor or radical correction.

In the June 23, 1992, issue of *The Mennonite,* an article by a member of the Ames (Iowa) Mennonite Fellowship was published advocating vegetarianism based on biblical principles. Published in the June 28 issue was an angry letter from a reader demanding that her subscription be canceled. She wrote, "There have been many times that I questioned some of the articles you have printed, but you have finally gone too far with this article."

Persons who give this kind of response to controversial articles are unable to exercise the principle of alternation—that is, to entertain the possibility that the alternative to what they believe to be true might in fact be true, whether or not it is true. The issue is not only the truth or error of any proposition, it is also whether or not church members can discuss any question with open minds and make a corporate discernment after hearing all sides. If there is ever withdrawal from the discernment process before the issue is fully discussed and resolved, the withdrawal should not be initiated by the side that has the truth.

There are many examples of the experience of alternation in the Bible itself. One example is in Mark 10:2-12. Some Pharisees approached Jesus with the declaration of Deuteronomy 24:1-4 that a man may divorce his wife by giving her a formal certificate of divorce. How, the Pharisees asked, did Jesus interpret this Scripture? Jesus replied, "Because of your hardness of heart he wrote this commandment for you. But from the beginning of creation, 'God made them male and female.'. . .Therefore what God has joined together, let no one separate."

Later the disciples asked Jesus for further interpretation. Was the passage in Deuteronomy not to be taken literally? Jesus replied that although Moses permitted divorce and remarriage because of the people's hardness of heart, divorce is always morally wrong.

Another question in the interpretation of the divorce texts arises from the fact that in the Matthew 5:32 parallel to the Mark 10 text, an exception is made for adultery. It is unlikely, however, that Jesus made any exception at all. His teaching was simply that "what God has joined together, let no one separate." In the process of trying to interpret this hard saying of Jesus, the early church added exceptions to his rule. If they did so with a sense of the leading of his Spirit, what they bound in particular cases was also bound in heaven, but the higher ideal remained.

The application of this teaching raises additional problems. One is that the increasing laxity with which divorce and remarriage is treated in the church today indicates how hard it is to apply the principle of alternation when it requires a shift from a permissive ethic to one that is absolute. On the other hand, suppose the issue in the church is unloving rejection of members who had reasonable motives for breaking up their marriage or are repentant for having divorced for questionable reasons. Then the discernment must in either case be made with proper respect for Jesus' teaching about the permanence of marriage. As Luke Johnson observes,

> Just as the church of today, the church of the first generation had to struggle at once with the seriousness of Jesus' demands, and the strictures of complex worldly existence. The church in every age must respond to the words of Jesus with creative fidelity. This does not mean a rigid or mechanical application, but a creative fidelity which means true obedience, and which translates the words accurately within changed social and religious structures. (Johnson, 94)

Another biblical example of the experience of alternation is the false messianic expectation followers of Jesus had of their Lord, an expectation shattered by the scandal of the cross and the subsequent scattering of the disciples in fear and confusion. The predominant view of the coming Messiah had been that of a royal king of the dynasty of David who would deliver Israel and reign triumphantly forever with the power of Yahweh. The amazing military successes of the Maccabees against the mad tyrannies of Antiochus Epiphanes had reinforced the hope for a nationalistic Messiah. If the occupying forces of the oppressor had been defeated once, why not again, once and forever, under the leadership of the anointed Messiah of God?

The early Christians could indeed identify many details of Jesus' life and ministry that seemed to match various prophecies alluding to such a messianic expectation. Jesus was born of the lineage of King David (Matt. 1:1; Ps. 89:3-4), he was baptized with the coronation formula from the "royal psalm" (Mark 1:11; Ps. 2:7), he came preaching the kingly rule of God (Mark 1:14-15; Isa.9:7), and he entered Jerusalem on the back of a donkey, the prophesied royal mount for the ruler of God's people (Mark 11:1-10; Zech. 9:9). Moreover, among Jesus' disciples were representatives of the party of the Zealots, whose zeal for Christ's kingdom was based on the expectation of the forceful overthrow of the Roman occupationary forces.

From the moment of Peter's confession at Caesarea Philippi, Jesus began an intensive dialogue with his disciples to correct their false expectations. Far from going to Jerusalem to overthrow the oppressors, he was going to suffer and be killed in fulfillment of the prophecies of Isaiah about a suffering servant Messiah (Isa. 53:1ff., etc.). Peter argued against this view, and Jesus rebuked him (Matt. 16:22).

The first post-resurrection Bible discussion continued this discernment process. Two disillusioned disciples on their way home, presumably to resume their old life, told the mysterious stranger on the road, "We had hoped that he was the one to redeem Israel" (Luke 24:21). The anonymous figure of the risen Lord replied,

> "Oh, how foolish you are, and how slow of heart to believe all that the prophets have declared! Was it not necessary that the Messiah should suffer these things and then enter into his glory?" Then beginning with Moses and all the prophets, he interpreted to them the things about himself in all the scriptures. (Luke 24:25-27)

From that point on, the early church implemented the principle of alternation and began to review the scriptural basis for a truer conception of the Messiah, the suffering Savior of the world. They began with the prophecies of Isaiah (Isa. 42:1ff.) and reexamined all other relevant Scripture passages through the lens of the transformational relationship of their new identity with the risen Christ (Green, 78-99). Then at last everything fell into place.

Their new discernment under the inspiration of the Advocate (see chapter 3) lasted about three centuries. Until the conversion of Emperor Constantine in A.D. 311, the early church adhered to the Lord's teachings about suffering love and nonresistance. Thereafter the Constantinian church reverted to a nonpacifist church-state ethic, so that even today it seems ironic that evangelical Christians who embrace a doctrine of biblical inerrancy do not really believe what Jesus taught about the way of suffering love and nonresistance (Matt. 16:24-27). They have become about as nationalistic as those early followers who expected Jesus to implement his kingdom through military power. And so the work of the Advocate continues to teach us and to bring to our remembrance all Jesus said to his disciples (John 14:26). We too are foolish disciples, slow of heart to believe (Luke 14:25).

In these two examples of alternation, we observe that biblical interpretation sometimes changes within the Scriptures themselves, not only when we move from the Old Testament to the New, but sometimes also when we move within the New Testament itself. This principle of alternation in no way undermines the authority of the Bible but emphasizes the importance of interpreting texts through the mind of Christ and in the perspective of the total sweep of the biblical narrative.

The Principles of Biblical Discernment

During the 1977 Mennonite General Assembly at Estes Park, Colorado, a position statement on "Biblical Interpretation in the Life of the Church" was adopted. The following principles are condensed and adapted from that statement (BI, 54-63).

> 1. *Jesus Christ is the Lord of Scripture.* What he said and did carries divine authority. Because he revealed the will of God, Jesus opens our eyes to understand the Scriptures (Luke 24:25). His life, obedient suffering, death, and resurrection are our guide for interpreting the Bible.
>
> 2. *The Holy Spirit enables the reader to understand the Bible.* The Spirit gives life to the written words. Only as the Word penetrates our lives, and its message is personally appropriated, does the text become living and powerful. When a Scripture becomes a living truth, is related to other texts, and then is understood within the larger framework of the biblical message, the Bible has meaning and authority. The Spirit thus witnesses to the authority of Scripture.
>
> 3. *The Bible is the book of the people of God.* The at-homeness of the Bible in the community of faith speaks to the issue of biblical authority. Unfor-

tunately, the Bible and the church are often seen as constrasting authorities. The unique authority and rule of God in Christ set forth in the Bible can become apparent only in the voluntary faith and obedience of the responding community.

4. *It is the task of each member to participate in the interpretation of the Bible.* We believe God gives special insight to individuals as they read and study the Bible. These insights are to be tested in the community (1 Cor. 14:29; 2 Pet. 1:20-22). This testing of interpretations ultimately needs to involve the whole people of God—individuals, study groups, congregations, conferences, denominations, and wider church.

5. *Informed Bible students have a special role.* Informed students are those who have given themselves to the study and teaching of the Bible. The task of such students is not to dominate interpretation of the Word, but to exercise leadership in this area. With their help we should learn as much as possible about the historical, cultural, and linguistic background of the [texts and] narrative of the Bible. This knowledge should not diminish but increase the authority of the Bible in guiding our lives in accord with God's will.

6. *The New Testament is the fulfillment of the Old Testament.* The ancient covenant which God made with the Israelites at Sinai was based on God's saving action and the willing response of the people. It prepared for the new covenant based on God's new and decisive act in Christ (Jer. 31:31; Mark 14:24; Heb. 7:22). The Old Testament tells us of covenants of promise (Gen. 12:1-3; Exod. 19:5-6; Eph. 2:12). The New Testament tells us of the fulfillment of the promise (Matt. 5:17). The relation of the testaments, therefore, is best understood as one of promise and fulfillment.

7. *The kingdom of Christ supersedes the kingdoms of Israel.* The people of God in the Old Testament, with God as Ruler (Judg. 3:22-23; 1 Sam. 8:7), were experiencing something of the kingdom of God; [but] Jesus the Messiah came to establish a new phase of God's kingdom on earth. Christ's kingdom has a spiritual and a social character. The ultimate fulfillment of the kingdom is yet to come, but Christ is Lord now in the life of believers (Acts 2:36; 1 Cor. 15:24; Rev. 11:15). The Bible speaks of two kingdoms, the kingdom of God and the kingdom of this world. The believer belongs to Christ's kingdom. Loyalty to this kingdom is absolute, making believers strangers and pilgrims in this world.

Summary and Conclusion

There will likely be an intense ongoing dialogue in our churches between the 78% of the members who believe that the Bible is the "inerrant Word of God" and the 16% who have doubts about the claim of biblical inerrancy (but also believe the Bible is the authoritative Word of God and a reliable guide for faith and life). However, the larger unresolved question is whether or not the members of both groups are using the Bible "to deal with the real problems of actual living persons in their daily lives," as Walter Wink put it.

In this chapter we discussed the principle of alternation and examined reasons why the doctrine of scriptural inerrancy may be questionable to some members. Jesus certainly had a high view of Scripture when he said to his disciples, "Not an iota, not a dot, will pass from the law until all is accomplished" (Matt. 5:18, RSV). But when he told the Pharisees that for their hardness of heart Moses wrote them this commandment permitting a man to divorce his wife at will (Mark 10:5), he was hardly describing Deuteronomy 24:1-4 as inerrant in the sense in which fundamentalists mean it—that every verse of the Bible is the flawless Word of God. For a growing number of members today, inerrancy is not a helpful way to talk about the authority, inspiration, and trustworthiness of the Scriptures.

The Bible is authoritative when the people of God read it with the mind of Christ. Then they find its message to be profoundly true, whether they move from the Bible to their lives for insight, or from their personal and interpersonal questions to the Bible for guidance.

In short, the question of biblical authority cannot be separated from the mandate that Christ gave to his church to bind and loose, to forgive and to retain sins, and to discern what the Advocate (the abiding Spirit of Jesus) is saying to his people in their ongoing search for guidance (John 14:16-17, 26; 16:7-14). It is in the fellowship of a discerning congregation that the Bible can be said to be the inspired Word of God, for it speaks God's Word to the people of God as they discern together what God would have them be and do.

We learn how the Scriptures become self-correcting when we observe this searching, revealing, reproving, and correcting process within the biblical narratives themselves. When we read how Christ reproved the Pharisees (Mark 10:5) or how one leader of the early church reproved another (Gal. 2:11), the Bible teaches us truthfully that marriage is always meant to be permanent and that in Christ there is neither Jew nor Greek "for all of you are one in Christ Jesus" (Gal. 3:28).

Some biblical scholars speak of the authority of the Bible primarily in terms of making intellectual sense out of our personal lives (Friesen, 30-1). In this chapter we have tried to say that the Bible has authority not only for personal discernment but also for corporate discernment in the fellowship of the church.

The biblical congregation meets under the authority of the Word and Spirit of God to discern what the Lord wants to say to us about the faith and life issues of our time. Such a community will be called to acts of loving service and mission as a continuing fulfillment of the preeminent love and suffering service of our Lord himself.

Discussion Questions

1. Do you believe that if we take the Bible seriously enough, we will find answers to our deepest questions about the meaning of life and death?

2. Which of the following CMP statements comes closest to expressing what you believe about the Bible? a. The Bible is the divinely inspired and inerrant Word of God, the only trustworthy guide for faith and life. b. The Bible is the authoritative Word of God and a reliable guide but not inerrant. Tabulate your responses on the chalkboard and discuss. Do you agree with the author that the question of inerrancy is less important than the fact that both statements affirm the Bible as the authoritative guide for faith and life?

3. According to the Rule of Christ, how should you relate to a member of your church who holds to a different view of the Bible than you do?

4. What do you think of Swartley's comment that the biblical congregation can resolve difficult ethical issues even though persons with opposing positions can find biblical texts to "prove" their points of view?

5. Can you accept the principle of alternation—that the alternative to what you believe to be true may in fact be true? If so, name one belief or attitude in your congregation that may in fact be wrong? Name one within yourself.

6. What do you think are some causes of the rising divorce rate in Mennonite and Brethren in Christ congregations? How can the Advocate, the abiding presence of Jesus' Spirit, help us to apply his teaching on divorce in specific cases?

CHAPTER 5

Discernment in the Apostolic Church

And after Paul and Barnabas had no small dissension and debate with them,
Paul and Barnabas and some of the others were appointed to go up to Jerusalem
to discuss this question with the apostles and the elders.
—Acts 15:2

THE MEMBERS OF THE CHURCH AT ANTIOCH apparently felt that through their leaders they had access to decision making at the highest level in Jerusalem. Similarly, 82% of the members of the five participant CMP II denominations say that in their congregations most members have a part in making important congregational decisions. Percentages did not vary significantly between our four types of church. This bodes well for the suggestions of this chapter concerning discernment process and procedures. It says little, however, about what these important decisions are in the typical congregation. Denise Preheim, our liberal church representative, expressed concerns about this.

We have a congregational meeting in our church three times a year. At our annual meeting in January, we hear the reports of our pastor and commission chairpersons and elect new officers. In spring we appoint our delegates to the annual meetings of our district conference and consider other agenda brought by the church council. In fall we talk mostly about money, adopt the budget for the coming year, and get ready for the annual fund drive.

Our typical congregational agenda deals mostly with our own "housekeeping" matters—accepting minutes of the previous meeting, approving reports, deciding whether to make improvements in the church building and equipment, endless discussion of finances, and whatever else comes under the category of "new business."

In my clinical pastoral training, we had a standard admonition, "go for the depths." This was a prod to move beyond the superficial to issues that really mattered. I'd like to see us go for the depths in our congregational meetings. I'd like to see us formulate position papers on the issues to be discussed at our district and general conferences. I'd like to see us really tackle some of the problems I see almost every day in my professional counseling.

To implement Denise's suggestions would demand major review of congregational goals, bring new agenda to congregational meetings, and require new methods of processing agenda and making decisions. It could even cause restructuring of adult Sunday school classes so they would bring their agenda and their best thinking to the attention of the congregation. Applying Denise's ideas would also encourage individual members to raise for group discernment their own deeper questions about what it means to be faithful disciples of Christ.

A Scenario from the Early Church

One of Luke's stories about discernment in the early church was about the resolution of the Jew-Gentile question in the congregation at Antioch and in the conference at Jerusalem (Acts 10—15). If Jesus was truly Israel's Messiah (Matt. 16:16), if his church was truly the new covenant foretold by Jeremiah (31:3), and if Jesus really meant that "not one letter, not one stroke of a letter, will pass from the law until all is accomplished" (Matt. 5:18), then should not Gentile Christians accept and obey the laws, including circumcision, which Moses brought down from Sinai? Up to a crucial point in Luke's story, the mother church at Jerusalem (whose elder was the Lord's brother James and where Peter and John were apostles) was tending to say "yes" to the question.

The opposite view was represented by the apostles Paul and Barnabas, following their first missionary tour. The requirement of circumcision and kosher food restrictions made little sense to Gentile converts because these things would turn them into Jews. The issue was the means of salvation. Were they saved by circumcision and obedience to the law of Moses (Acts 15:1) or by the grace of Jesus Christ apart from works of the law (Acts 15:11)? Luke's narrative together with parts of Paul's letters provide important clues about how the early church processed this question. And the Acts account provides a model for us as we seek to discern all kinds of issues in our churches.

The Jew-Gentile issue came to a head at the Jerusalem Conference (Acts 15). Today we might say this discussion process was more like a district conference session than a congregational meeting, although it was the daughter church at Antioch that first processed the question, then brought it to the mother church for resolution. The Antioch church appointed Paul and Barnabas and other members to go process the issue with the apostles and elders in Jerusalem (Acts 15:2). On the basis of all that we know about the church at Antioch, we can reconstruct the congregational process that led to that decision.

The development of the church at Antioch (Acts 11:19ff.) is what we today call the "mother church-daughter church" model of church planting (L. Harder, B, 170-1). The persecution of Christians in Jerusalem had caused their dispersion; Antioch was one of their three destinations (v. 19). In character with the attitude of the mother church, the first believers to arrive in Antioch "spoke the word to no one except Jews" (v. 19).

When additional fugitives from Cyprus and Cyrene began to witness to Gentiles also (v. 20), the mother church sent Barnabas to unify these factions and exhort them all "to remain faithful to the Lord with steadfast devotion" (v. 23). Luke did not say whether "faithful to the Lord" also meant "faithful to the law of Moses"; that was surely one question Barnabas was sent to clarify. His assignment became a year-long teaching ministry to a growing assembly of people (v. 26). Needing assistance, Barnabas contacted Paul in Tarsus and brought him to Antioch to help with the teaching (v. 25-26). A nonbiblical source reports that the congregation met on Singon Street near the Pantheon (Downey, 147); Luke adds the interesting detail that "it was in Antioch that the disciples were first called 'Christians' " (v. 26).

Concerning the size of the group, Luke reports only that "a great number became believers and turned to the Lord" (v. 21) and that there were "a great many people" (v. 26). Apart from certain leaders identified by name, the group was composed of numerous anonymous "disciples" and "believers" (11:26; 14:28; 15:32-33). Those named were Barnabas, Paul, Symeon, Niger, Lucius of Cyrene (who may have been Luke, author of the gospel of Luke and the Acts of the Apostles), and Manaen, "a member of the court of Herod the ruler" (13:1).

Thus the church at Antioch was a mixture of ethnic groups and cultures. Several commentators speculate that the person who really got it started was not a Jewish Christian at all but a native Antiochan named Nicolaus, one of the seven deacons appointed at Jerusalem (6:5). Michael Green writes that "he may have preferred to go back home to share Christ . . . than to remain shut up with the apostles in Jerusalem" (Green, 114).

Luke's account suggests that while the entire congregation met together for the teaching of Paul and Barnabas, the Jewish Christians met separately for the communion meal. This was because they feared violating their taboos by associating with unclean Gentiles (Acts 10:28; Gal. 2:11-12; 1 Pet. 4:3-4) and eating meat that had come from animals sacrificed in the Syrian temple. Apparently there was a food shop in Antioch, connected with the Pantheon, where Gentiles bought groceries including fish and meat, the meat having been part of an animal previously sacrificed to a pagan god or idol.

The meat was nutritious enough for public consumption, and Paul approved its use by Christians (1 Cor. 10:25) unless it was eaten at a communal meal in the temple (vv. 20-21) or unless eating it proved a stumbling block to conscience-bound members (vv. 28-29, 8:1-13, especially v. 9). Luke tells of a delegation from Judea who came to Antioch to insist that Gentile believers be circumcised according to "the custom of Moses" (Acts 15:1) and that the rest of the law also be enforced on them (v. 5). Paul added several revealing details.

> But when Cephas [Peter] came to Antioch, I opposed him to his face, because he stood self-condemned; for until certain people came from James, he used to eat with the Gentiles. But after they came, he drew back and kept himself separate for fear of the circumcision faction. And the other Jews joined him in this hypocrisy, so that even Barnabas was led astray by their hypocrisy. But when I saw that they were not acting consistently with the truth of the gospel, I said to Cephas before them all, "If you, though a Jew, live like a Gentile and not like a Jew, how can you compel the Gentiles to live like Jews?" (Gal. 2:11-14)

With this background it is easy to imagine the Antioch congregation's discernment process. They gathered at their place of worship. The meeting was not formal but contained a structured freedom of participation for everyone (see 1 Cor. 14:26). Somebody could always be counted on to repeat some Jesus story, and another would lead a hymn. One would give a prophecy and another would have an admonition. They would eat and drink the Lord's Supper, then share whatever food they had brought at a common meal.

At this point a number of the Jewish believers were tending to withdraw to eat as a subgroup. We can imagine that on one of these occasions there was a conversation like this one.

> **Nicolaus:** I urge you for the Lord's sake not to disperse until we have eaten the meal together, for our Lord prayed that we would always be united.
> **Levi:** How is it possible to eat the meal together when there is meat on the table purchased at the Pantheon?
> **Reuben:** And how can we eat the meal together before Lucius and Manaen have submitted to circumcision like you, Nicolaus, before you were ordained a deacon in Jerusalem?

In the discussion that followed, different perspectives or attitudes needed to be expressed and processed if there was to be any conflict resolution, discernment, and consensus. Such diversity had to be accepted as a natural part of the process, not to be avoided and ignored by subtle forms of withdrawal. Members in disagreement needed to acknowledge the tension within the group and within each member, for each wanted both to cling to what he or she believed to be true and be open to the possibility an alternative view might in fact be true. This kind of honest approach to discernment is possible only if members have truly covenanted to be led by the Advocate, the abiding Spirit of Jesus always present when his people gather (John 14:15-17).

There was, first, the perspective of the party of the Pharisees (Acts 15:5), also called the circumcision party (11:2). In the vocabulary of twentieth-century group dynamics, we might call this the perspective of the *reactionary*. Such a person works for a return to some prior system of faith and life. Before coming to Antioch, members of the party of the Pharisees were simply conservatives (see below), but now they had to advocate a return to a once accepted yet now threatened style of faith and life. Listen as we imagine what these reactionary Jewish Christians had to say in Antioch.

> **Levi:** If we as a church claim to stand on the promises of Abraham, Isaac, and Jacob, the only course open to us is to return to the Laws of the old covenant given by Yahweh. Compromise now means surrender later on.
> **Reuben:** Didn't Yahweh command circumcision? Does Yahweh change? Was not our Lord circumcised? Did he not come first to the lost sheep of the house of Israel? Did he not say that he came not to abolish the law?
> **Nicodem:** Back to the Scriptures! The Scriptures say, "Know therefore that the Lord your God is God, the faithful God who maintains covenant loyalty with those who love him and keep his commandments, to a thousand generations, and who repays in their own person those who reject him. . . .Therefore, observe diligently the commandments—the statutes, and the ordinances—that I am commanding you today" [Deut.7:9-11].
> **Reuben:** Is there any argument to justify the fellowship of the children of the covenant with the children of darkness unless they too enter by the narrow gate and walk the hard way, as both Moses and our Lord Jesus Christ commanded?

As we listen to these arguments, we cannot easily dismiss the logic of their position. "It was theologically respectable. . . . In fact, the weight of the evidence would seem to be on their side" (Johnson, 80). Often in the process of congregational discernment, we get carried away with the arguments of only one side when forcefully presented. Paul compared that with being "tossed to and fro and blown about by every wind of doctrine" (Eph. 4:14). The reactionary suffers from need to withdraw, to divide, to separate. There is a sense in which separation is biblical (Isa. 52:11; 2 Cor. 6:17)—but only as a spiritual, not a geographical or physical separation. It is more biblical to say that "if there must be a break within the church between the unfaithful church and the faithful church, the initiative must come from the unfaithful side" (Yoder, A, 33).

There is, secondly, the attitude of the *conservative*. This person resists rapid changes if they seem to threaten the preservation of traditional values. Conservatives do not oppose gradual changes which in the long run may lead to substantial transformation, but they oppose radical changes that might introduce foreign elements from the surrounding culture. Again we can imagine arguments of the conservatives in Antioch.

> **Simeon:** In the Lord's own time, before there was any thought of a Christian congregation in Antioch, the Lord was working out his fulfillment of the old covenant gradually and surely, first to the Jew and then to the Gentile, but all in the fullness of time, preserving tradition while remaining open to gradual change.
>
> **Barnabas:** To the Syrophoenician woman he said, "Let the children be fed first, for it is not fair to take the children's food and throw it to the dogs," to which the woman replied, "Sir, even the dogs under the table eat the children's crumbs" [Mark 7:27-28]. And for her faith, her daughter was healed, for the time for her healing had come. But has the time yet arrived for the barriers between Jew and Gentile to be torn down by the abolition of circumcision and the rest of our sacred traditions?
>
> **Nicolaus:** You have a point, Simeon and Barnabas. We dare not pretend there is no dividing wall between Jew and Gentile. I, a Gentile, was circumcised; you cannot now uncircumcise me with a resolution. Lucius is uncircumcised, and he refuses to be altered. To bridge these differences is a beautiful vision for the future, but it cannot be changed all at once.
>
> One thing I know, however, is that once I was lost in the darkness of this fallen world. Then a friend told me about the good news of Christ's kingdom. It spoke to my predicament.
>
> When I cried out, "What must I do to be saved?" he said, "Believe in the Lord Jesus, and you will be saved."
>
> I believed, and it brought such a wonderful hope into my life that I wanted to become a part of the new Israel, even to the point of being circumcised—although I now see more clearly that we are saved by the grace of the Lord Jesus Christ and not by tradition.

The conservative guards tradition from the past. The word *tradition* presents a bit of a problem for the conservative, because other traditions have probably already infiltrated the conservative's own tradition at any given time. Nevertheless, the conservative echoes the words of Paul, "Test everything; hold fast to what is good" (1 Thess. 5:21). The problem with the conservative stance is that it lays the burden of proof for any change on the backs of others. The conservative also fails to acknowledge the degree to which the gospel is essentially transformational and not just dedicated to maintain things as they are.

The third position is that of the *progressive*. Progressives work for changes that can be effected by orderly discernment and decision making. They try to clarify the issue in question, to determine what seems possible, and to translate vague general goals into operational, measurable objectives. In the Antioch congregation, the progressives probably suggested a number of specific objectives.

> **Deborah:** Let us pray that Levi, Reuben, and Nicodem will be able to bring our separated members back into our fold, if not today at least by the end of the year.
>
> **Priscilla:** Let us ask Simeon to talk with Asher, whom we know is rigidly orthodox in keeping every jot and dot of the law, for they seem to have a relationship of trust with each other. Perhaps he can help Asher see that Jesus was Lord also of the Scriptures.
>
> **Lucius:** Let us ask our sister, Tryphaena, to speak with Lydia when she returns from Seleucia, concerning her questionable mixture of the teachings of Paul and Barnabas with the doctrines of the mystery cults.
>
> **Deborah:** Let us each one this week add our Lord's prayer for the unity of his church to our daily devotions.
>
> **Sophia:** Let us ask Barnabas and Paul to lead us in a study of the true relationship between the new covenant and the old, for even as they were on the way back from their mission, the Spirit of the Lord was revealing many truths to them about this.
>
> **Barnabas:** We should take our concerns in this matter to the apostles and elders in Jerusalem, for it was their people who came here and provoked our Jewish brethren to withdraw.
>
> **Paul:** Let us also remain open to their concerns about this matter of eating meat sacrificed to idols and show our good faith to them by taking relief funds to their impoverished brethren.

None of these suggestions decisively solved the Jew-Gentile conflict, but all moved in the direction of resolution. There is something refreshing about the progressive spirit. It is free to change and free from an inhibiting cultural lag. It is marked by a realism that works on the possible and does not get hung up by what seems impossible. Progressives are basically optimistic about moving forward into history. They are confident everything will turn out all right if only we clarify our goals, translate them into measurable objectives, and work on one goal at a time. At times, however, the attitude of the progressive seems naively confident that proper goal-setting will guarantee progress, lacking awareness that progress cannot always be programmed.

There is typically also a fourth position, that of the *radical*. The radical demands speedy, deep, thorough change. We can imagine several friends of Tryphaena turning to Paul and Barnabas.

> **Julia:** What I hear you say, Barnabas, is that the elders in Jerusalem have the final word on these matters. I think we should settle the matter for ourselves right here in Antioch.

Olympia: You said to us, Paul, that you preach nothing but Christ and him crucified, but now I hear you adding something to your gospel—abstinence from meat that comes from the Pantheon food store.

Manaen: The women are right! If we are justified by faith and not by works of the law as you've been teaching, I see no value at all in abstaining from the temple meat. The meat is good, and we know that an idol has no real existence, for there is no God but the Father of our Lord Jesus Christ. It's time to end this nonsense about all the Jewish food restrictions and get on with our mission! Let's act on our new knowledge and not be sidetracked by the old. As you taught us, Paul, "all things have been made new, and the old has already passed away."

The radical is the preeminent change agent. The radical is a prophet who calls the community of faith to move ahead with its agenda, to live in the freedom of new-found faith, to include persons of other races and backgrounds, to share limited material resources, and to oppose compromises in belief or ethics. But radicals also have a problem. They are often basically angry. If they grew up in impoverished homes, the anger they now vent on the affluent community is understandable. If they grew up in middle- or upper-class homes, the frustrations they are displacing on the community may be an unconscious rebellion against authority figures. They may be unaware that they fight the establishment, not because they are so righteous, but because they never made peace with authoritarian fathers or leaders.

The reader familiar with Acts 15 knows how this discernment process turned out. The Antiochan congregation sent Paul and Barnabas to the apostles and elders in Jerusalem to consult about these questions (v. 2). As they were graciously welcomed, they told about the marvelous ways God was moving among the Gentiles to take out of them a people for his name. But they also protested the way representatives of the party of the Pharisees had come from Jerusalem to insist that "it is necessary for them to be circumcised and ordered to keep the law of Moses" (Acts 15:5).

The apostles and elders convened a conference "to consider this matter" (v. 6). Various points of view were offered, not unlike some of those expressed at Antioch, except that in the presence of leaders like Peter and James another level of authority was at work. Although James had previously expressed a reactionary attitude and Peter had vacillated between a progressive and a conservative stance (Gal. 2:12), they were all now caught up by the intervention of the Holy Spirit (Acts 15:28). The result was the Jerusalem declaration (vv. 23-29), about which everyone rejoiced, both in Jerusalem and in Antioch (v. 31).

Service Abilities in the Discernment Process

The discernment experience at Antioch impacted Paul's subsequent work as a church planter in Asia Minor and Europe. Although he specifically mentions the Antioch experience only once in his letters (Gal. 2:11ff.), his frequent references to gifts of the Spirit (Rom. 12:6; 1 Cor. 12:4; Eph. 4:11) undoubtedly reflect the experience of the church that ordained him for this work.

Paul's word *charismata* can be translated "spiritual gifts," "grace gifts," or more loosely "service abilities." In the words of Romans 12:6-8,

> We have gifts that differ according to the grace given to us: prophecy, in proportion to faith; ministry, in ministering; the teacher, in teaching; the exhorter, in exhortation; the giver, in generosity; the leader, in diligence; the compassionate, in cheerfulness.

Those service abilities applicable to the discernment process throw additional light on that process from a Pauline perspective. They have to do with prophetic admonitions, competent teaching, and sensitive exhortation. The discernment process has to do with the nature of authority in the body of Christ and how it is exercised by the members. Authority in the body of Christ refers to the divine right of members to admonish, serve, teach, and exhort one another according to each one's ability.

When discussing procedure, we should distinguish between authority and authoritarianism. Authority refers to mutual influence under valid biblical-theological safeguards. Authoritarianism refers to influence imposed without these safeguards.

These are the biblical-theological criteria:

Authority comes from God. Authority is not essentially vested in the person with the most knowledge or education or popularity but is given by God to a group of Christians by a process of continuing revelation, discernment, and consensus (Matt. 16:19; John 16:12-13). God's word on any subject under discussion is a discernible message. Alternative points of view need to be expressed, but differences of opinion indicate that God's word still needs to be more fully discerned. Differences may mean everybody is grasping part—but not all—of God's word.

Or it may be, even when everyone is in agreement, that nobody is discerning God's word if the hard work of searching for God's word has been short-circuited. But if the members are truly open to know God's word, have searched the Scriptures, studied their history, rehearsed their theology, and listened to testimony, they can trust the Holy Spirit to enlighten their minds, helping them to discern the mind of Christ.

Authority comes through each one. In the church's discernment process, every member participates according to the grace gifts and service abilities God has bestowed. All persons can make contributions on several levels of participation related to how much the Spirit enables them to mediate the word of God and speak with authority.

At the most common level of the discernment process, a participant can share an opinion. It is always important to let the group know how an idea under discussion appears to a participant as the group moves from early stages of interaction toward consensus. Differences of opinion should be accepted graciously, not as signs of irreconcilable dissension but as steps toward reaching consensus. Disagreement may be the very factor that brings the group together for discernment (Acts 15:1ff.). And some conflict between various conservative, progressive, radical, and reactionary points of view is to be expected.

At the same time, we should always acknowledge that God's word is greater than anyone of us grasps on first deliberation, and that our first opinion may be wide of the mark. If the principle of alternation is understood by all, the group can permit wide variance of opinions to be expressed without prejudging or pigeon-holing anyone.

At a higher level of the discernment process, members can exercise the service abilities they have from God to move the group toward consensus (1 Cor. 12:7). One needed service ability is knowing how to reflect another person's statement of opinion in the hearer's own words to test whether the speaker is being heard correctly, and then to enable the group to test the validity of the opinion (1 Cor. 12:10). Speakers will often restate their position in better terms when helped by others to see how they were heard in the first place.

Another service ability is to hold the group to the exploration of one strand of thought until the discussion reaches greater clarity or resolution. Unselfish service to the discernment process often requires humble willingness to postpone expression of opinion until others have been helped to incorporate their views into the discernment process.

Authority comes through gifted leaders. Leadership in the discernment process is a special service ability bestowed by God. It is a special type of authority through which God's authority is mediated. Some are given the ability to speak directly for God, in the name of Jesus, concerning the subject under discussion. Jesus did this superbly and was uniquely able to speak "as one having authority and not as the scribes" (Mark 1:22). Throughout the history of the church, certain persons have emerged in every congregation who bear Jesus' likeness to speak God's word on a certain question and to help the rest move forward. Such leadership may come formally from appointed group leaders or informally from one of the members. In either case, true leadership in the church is not an office to which a person is elected but a service to the group process authenticated by the gift of grace within.

The central point in all this talk of discernment is the desire to move from superficiality in the Christian faith to the deeper depths of discipleship and to discover what the Lord is saying to a congregation about issues and resources for addressing them. If Christ is not a living reality in the congregation, it is beside the point to discuss methods and procedures that presume he is Lord.

Summary and Conclusion

In this chapter we examined the Antiochan congregation as a case study of congregational discernment. From our twentieth-century perspective, we can see that the resolution of the Jew-Gentile question was a wonderful move in the direction of universalizing the church. We can also readily affirm that the resolution was indeed led by the Holy Spirit.

It should now be more evident to us that the gospel of Jesus Christ is fundamentally transformational. In principle if not always in practice, the gospel is a constant influence for change. Potentially if not immediately, the gospel makes all things new. At any given time, church members who are serious about following Jesus should be ready to change from the ways of this world to the ways of the kingdom of heaven.

We observed four perspectives at work in the Antiochan discernment process in relation to change. The conflict among the parties had more to do with the preferred direction and timing of change than with promotion of or resistance to change. All four points of view contributed to the resolution of the Jew-Gentile question. The Jerusalem Conference would not likely have moved to abolish the requirement of circumcision unless strong *radical* influence had been brought to bear and the *progressives* had been willing to negotiate with the *conservatives* on the matter of dietary restrictions. The Conference would not likely have brought the *reactionaries* along if their basic position that the new covenant was indeed grounded in the old had not been fully respected. And the *radicals* might have rejected any compromise had they not been helped to see the validity of the reactionary position—that even as we move forward we have to reaffirm our roots.

The decision made at the Jerusalem Conference was a compromise—a concession on the part of the *reactionaries* on the issue of circumcision and a reciprocal concession on the part of the *radicals* on the issue of abstaining from offensive practices. The overriding benefit of the compromise was that now Jew and Gentile could work together in a united Christian church. Most Christians today no longer feel bound to abstain from meat that has been strangled, but we can readily conclude that this part of the resolution was God's will for that time and situation, if not necessarily for ours. Discernment is sometimes like that for the sake of reconciliation and conflict resolution. This should warn us against becoming legalistic on one hand, or on the other hand prematurely concluding that God's word in every situation is always a concession to conflicting points of view among his people.

The Bible remains amazingly helpful in addressing problems of conflict and change among the people of God. Much of the New Testament was written by Paul, whom some would call a radical and others a conservative. In his epistles, we would likely find evidence that he saw truth in all four attitudes, all of them needed in the discernment process in the body of Christ. "Now there are varieties of gifts, but the same Spirit; and there are varieties of services, but the same Lord; and there are varieties of activities, but it is the same God who activates all of them in everyone. To each is given the manifestation of the Spirit for the common good" (1 Cor. 12:4-8).

Paul was critical of those Christian brothers and sisters who maintained their attitude to the point of dividing the church. He claimed to be the most free of the free, to be able to eat and drink with liberty without violating his own conscience, but he said, "If food is a cause of their falling, I will never eat meat, so that I may not cause one of them to fall" (1 Cor. 8:13).

Based on his experience in Antioch and other churches he helped plant, Paul admonished members to consider the service abilities given them by the Spirit "for building up the body of Christ, until all of us come to the unity of the faith and of the knowledge of the Son of God, to maturity [and] to the measure of the full stature of Christ" (Eph. 4:12b-13).

We have not always been fully aware of how important Christian unity was to Jesus and the early apostles—not uniformity of attitude, because we have different gifts and different points of view, but unity of purpose and partnership in discerning what we as disciples are to believe and do.

Discussion Questions

1. How would you answer this two-choice CMP question: In my church ____most members have a part in making the important congregational decisions; ____most members do not have much part in the church's decision-making process. Tabulate the answers on the chalkboard and discuss.

2. On a scale from 1 to 10 (from superficial agenda to really important agenda), how would you rate the typical agenda of your church at congregational meetings? Tabulate the responses and discuss.

3. If you had been a member of the Antioch congregation, what

would likely have been your attitude on the Jew-Gentile question: ____Reactionary. ____Conservative. ____Progressive. ____Radical. ____A combination of all four. Can a congregation contain persons of all four types and still enjoy healthy fellowship?

4. Are you a good listener? If so, do you feed back what you think you are hearing? How many members of a discussion group really do this?

5. Is it possible for all in a congregation to agree about some moral-ethical issue, yet for none to be truly discerning God's word?

Discernment of the Call to Faith

CHAPTER 6

How Is Faith Formed and Integrated?

. . . until all of us come . . . to maturity,
to the measure of the full stature of Christ.
—Ephesians 4:13

IN THIS PASSAGE Paul was referring not just to the maturity of individual members but to the maturity of the church—"all of us." To be sure, every Christian is called to maturity in Christ. But no one can attain mature faith without sharing in the fullness of Christ in the congregation.

The question posed by our chapter heading was the subject of a recent national study conducted by the Search Institute in Minneapolis on behalf of six Protestant denominations and entitled "Effective Christian Education." In this chapter we will examine several findings from this study in relation to our own CMP research data and use this and other writings as sources for our own discernment of how faith is formed and integrated.

What Makes Faith Mature?

That was the title of an article summarizing the Search Institute study, the findings of which are generally sobering.

> Visit any mainline Sunday school class and you will probably find only a smattering of adults and high school students. The students will seem bored and uninvolved, the teacher burned-out and ill-equipped. Then follow some church members through the week. Few will show any signs that they are Christians. They won't participate in rallies to fight injustice or discrimination. People in mainline churches live lives unaffected by their faith. And part of the problem is that churches are not doing what it takes to make faith mature. (Roehrlkepartain, 496)

The researchers began their study by defining the characteristics of a mature faith. "A person of mature faith experiences both a life-transforming relationship to a loving God—the vertical theme—and a consistent devotion to others—the horizontal theme" (Benson/Eklin, 10). The researchers designed a questionnaire to measure four characteristics of the vertical dimension—

> trusts in God's saving grace and believes firmly in the humanity and divinity of Jesus;
> experiences the fruits of faith: personal well-being, security, and peace;
> seeks spiritual growth through study, reflection, prayer, and discussion with others;
> integrates faith and life, seeing work, family, social relationships, and political choices as part of one's religious life.

The researchers also measured four characteristics of the horizontal dimension—

> seeks to be a part of a community of believers in which people witness to their faith and support and nourish one another;
> holds life-affirming values, including a commitment to racial and gender equality, an affirmation of cultural and religious diversity, and a personal sense of responsibility for the welfare of others;
> advocates social and global change to bring about greater social justice;
> serves humanity consistently and passionately through acts of love and justice. (Benson/Eklin, 10)

A member who scored high on both dimensions was judged to have a *mature or integrated faith*. Low scores on one or the other of the dimensions indicated an *underdeveloped faith*. Low scores on both dimensions indicated an *undeveloped faith*. The survey of over 11,000 members of 561 mainline Protestant congregations revealed that about 32% of those questioned had an integrated mature faith, 32% had an underdeveloped faith, and 36% had an undeveloped faith. Of those with an underdeveloped faith, 69% scored low in the vertical dimension and 31% scored low on the horizontal dimension.

Although the Mennonite and Brethren in Christ CMP research project was conducted without reference to the Search Institute study, our questionnaire gauged similar characteristics of mature horizontal and vertical faith. On nine selected measurements roughly comparable between the two studies, CMP respondents scored significantly higher on both dimensions overall. The one exception was personal evangelism— members of Mennonite and Brethren in Christ churches find it difficult to talk with other people about their faith.

We also discovered that our members of separatist type churches tend to score comparatively higher on the vertical dimension but lower on the horizontal dimension. Conversely, members of the liberal churches tend to score comparatively higher on the horizontal dimension but lower on the vertical dimension.

Which of the four types of churches might be most functional for the development of a mature integrated faith according to the Search Institute criterion of scoring high on both dimensions? The transformist church scored first or second in six vertical and seven horizontal items and was the only type that showed that kind of balance and integration.

It is not difficult to surmise why this might be so. Transformist churches tend to be newly formed congregations in urban centers with renewed commitment to the Anabaptist vision. This commitment is often made explicit in the form of a written covenant in which members try to preserve the best in their religious heritage while discarding elements found dysfunctional for their faith and life in the city. The level of education of members is higher than for the other three types, and their church tends to be a small fellowship in which most members are likely to be active participants.

In transformist settings the old Sunday school model with closely graded classes is not feasible. A different style of nurture is developed in the context of an intergenerational group that often meets as a whole for worship, mutual support, and discernment of issues. In the process of sharing personal struggles, giving and receiving counsel, and making decisions about their corporate life and mission as Christians, members of transformist churches learn how to deal with their differences and strive on toward consensus.

Some of these factors were expressed in our interview with Menno Isaac.

> Almost half of the people in our Escarpment Fellowship are single young adults—university students, graduates beginning careers in the city, MCC trainees, and our Voluntary Service unit. For all of these people who regularly attend the midweek Bible study and prayer meeting in our home, this is a support group in which each can give and receive support.
>
> I think of one person in particular—a sensitive, gifted young adult from an affluent Anglican family in Toronto. He had a degree in architecture from the University of Toronto but was quickly disillusioned by the tendencies of his professional colleagues to cater to the rich in our society and to exploit the limited energy resources without concern about depletion and extravagance. He went back to the University and earned a second degree in special education.
>
> Then he rode his bicycle all the way to Hamilton to teach in a school for emotionally disturbed children. Day after day, week after week, he gave himself to a difficult and often hostile group of teenagers. In our weekly prayer meeting, he would share the experiences of the week—some hope-

ful and some discouraging, and we would pray for him and for the children. One Wednesday evening when he felt like celebrating some little break-through with one of his students, he said, "This Fellowship is my rock! I wouldn't make it through the week if it wasn't for the support of all of you!"

One time when we were working our way through the Gospel of Matthew, we came to chapter 16, where Jesus told his disciples that he would give them the keys to the kingdom of heaven and whatever they bound on earth would be bound in heaven. This seemed to refer also to us and our right to make binding decisions.

It was about the time that refugees from El Salvador were coming to Canada in search for asylum. For weeks news of their desperate plight came to us through the media, and for weeks we had prayed for them. At one of our midweek meetings, the subject came up again, and it was evident that it was becoming more frustrating to pray for them if we didn't also try to do something.

I moderated a quick process of discernment, and we decided there and then to contact a local refugee agency. The next day the person we had asked (or should I say, "bound") to make the contact called to report that the agency wanted us to sponsor a Salvadoran couple who were already in Hamilton. So we went to work to find an apartment, gather furniture, and share the many tasks and moneys needed to help one Salvadoran couple in all of their adjustments to a new city. It took some doing, but our spirits were high as we worked together on this special mission.

Working together on a project like this as part of their study and teaching of the Bible is an integral part of the members' (and their children's) nurture as Christians.

How Is Faith Developed?

In his book, *Will Our Children Have Faith?* John Westerhoff speaks of faith as a verb, as "a way of behaving which involves knowing, being, and willing" (Westerhoff, 89). Following the life cycle stages of faith development as formulated by James Fowler, Westerhoff describes four styles of faith. The first is *experienced faith*, by which preschool and school-age children imbibe a style of trusting, believing, praying, and loving in an environment of trust with other younger and older "faithing selves" (Westerhoff, 93).

The second is the *affiliative faith* of adolescents who move to a more independent voluntary sense of belonging to the faith community. This normally follows a gradual process of Christian education in Sunday schools leading to confirmation or catechism classes as preparation for baptism and membership in the church.

The third style is the *searching faith* of Christians who in late teen and young adult years react with new doubt and critical judgments about their earlier understandings of faith. They will tend to be more willing to experiment with alternative styles, testing the tradition of their past by trying other options. "It is only then that they are able to reach convictions which are truly their own" (Westerhoff, 97) and eventually make more mature commitments to God and to the church.

The fourth style is the *owned faith* of later adulthood, when persons want and need to make more enduring, comprehensive, life-embracing commitments to Christ and his church.

Following is another model of the "faithing" process, but with several important differences (L. Harder, F, 347-358). The faith of mature, well-integrated Christians develops over the life span as a result of four life cycle educational methods: nurture, instruction, proving, and discipleship as follows:

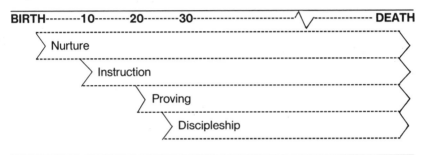

Nurture, which begins at birth and continues throughout the lifespan, is largely the unconscious acceptance of Christian beliefs and attitudes through constant interaction with peers and elders in the Christian community. As we read in Deuteronomy 6:4-7, nurture was the main method by which faith was developed in early Israel.

Horace Bushnell, a nineteenth-century New England theologian, took this Old Testament image of nurture and interpreted it in a way that has greatly influenced the religious education movement. Bushnell used two arguments to support his thesis that "the child is to grow up a Christian and never know himself as being otherwise" (Bushnell, 4). The first was the organic unity argument that the values and character of the fostering group is propagated in its children as naturally and by a law as truly organic as when the sap of the trunk flows into a limb. Second, Bushnell argued that the bonding between the members of the Christian family and community is like that of the ancient covenant between Yahweh and his people.

Nurture has certainly been the predominant method of faith formation among Mennonites. In the language of Bushnell, John Oyer writes that "there has never been a time in my life when I was not a Christian in some sense of the word, and even more particularly a Mennonite" (Oyer,

182). Among those who wrote for the book *Why I Am a Mennonite,* this theme occurs repeatedly.

> "Why am I a Mennonite? Largely, I suppose, because I was born into a Mennonite home and raised in a Mennonite community."—Gordon D. Kaufman (Loewen, 127)
> "I am a Mennonite because my parents were. I suspect that most of us who share our stories here would have to begin with that simple acknowledgment."—Walter Klaassen (Loewen, 141)
> "Growing up in a Russian-Mennonite village and only vaguely remembering the last church service before all the churches were closed by the Soviet government, my early contacts with Mennonitism could come only through the home. I am sure that the teaching of my parents had some impact on me, but what I really remember are the behavior and actions of family members in that given situation."—George K. Epp (Loewen, 51)
> "An important factor for me being Mennonite was that I was born into a Mennonite home, grew up in a Mennonite community, and discovered my first conscious religious ideas within a Mennonite setting. In a real sense, my being Mennonite was a gift. It was not earned, nor chosen, but given."
> —John Friesen (Loewen, 91)

The weakness of the nurture method of faith development is what Peter Berger calls "the propagation of bad faith" (Berger, A, 87ff.) within a family or community that has lost its direction as the people of God. This happened to the ancient Israelites in their adoption of Baal worship (Sherrill, 37-41).

Bad faith has also befallen Mennonites, as Rudy Wiebe's novels have so poignantly portrayed. In *Peace Shall Destroy Many,* Thom Wiens has been well nurtured in the faith of his pacifist community; but in the course of one year, he comes to see how much lovelessness, legalism, and hypocrisy characterizes the social and religious life of his community under the moralistic influence of Deacon Block (R. Wiebe, 238ff.). The hypocrisy of Mennonite nurture is also the theme of a poem by Peter Ediger.

Blindness
In a community where
Jesus loved the little children of the
world red and yellow black and white
and four letter words were not thought of let alone
spoken and toy guns were never pointed at
people a sling shot was called a
nigger-shooter. (P. Ediger,22)

In a devastating critique of the religious establishment in America, Peter Berger shows how typical religious nurture today provides the individual with the means by which he can hide from himself the true nature of his existence. Religion reassures and strengthens him in his social roles, however "inauthentic" these may be. Religion thus tends to become an obstacle in the progress towards "authenticity" as a person. (Berger, B, 102)

This leads historically and biographically to the second method of faith development, that of *instruction*—the formal study of the Bible and other Christian literature, usually in schools established for this purpose, including the Sunday church school.

We find a biblical instance of this faith development process in 2 Kings 22 and 23. Josiah became king of Judah and during his thirty-one year reign a great reformation happened. The altars of the Baals were destroyed and the temple restored. While this was happening, a roll of scriptural manuscript was discovered. When Josiah had finished reading it, he was so shaken by a sense of its authority that he rent his clothes. He called for an assembly of all the people to hear the words of the Lord which had been found in the house of the Lord. We read that the people followed Josiah in renewing the covenant with their Lord to walk in obedience to his commandments as written in the rediscovered book of Law.

The publication of this document (perhaps the book of Deuteronomy) around the year 621 B.C. was one of the great landmarks in the history of Judah, whose religion henceforth became a religion of a book. After the Exile, Ezra regularly assembled the people to instruct them from the book of the Law, committing them more deeply to a book as the Word of God. Then schools were established to instruct the young people in the Scriptures to make them wise about salvation and participation in the covenant community of God.

The redeeming role of instruction is well illustrated in the *Why I Am a Mennonite* essays. Hedy Martens speaks for many when she writes,

> In my teenage years we moved to Manitoba, where I attended Mennonite Collegiate Institute in Gretna. It was probably here, through the study of Mennonite history, that I first began to form an articulate separation between my ethnic identity and my religious identity, and where I began to become more fully aware of the distinctive [character] of the Mennonite (Anabaptist) way of interpreting and living Scripture. (Loewen, 169)

Christian instruction is another crucial way faith takes root and grows, especially when the curriculum is "the strange new world of the Bible" as Karl Barth put it. Unless the Bible is rediscovered in the lives of each of us in some similar manner, our faith too will not mature, for the Bible is the locus of our own encounter with the revelation events of our faith. The Bible is where we meet the historical Jesus and read his teachings about God's kingdom.

The perversion of Christian instruction comes at the point when a fundamentalist doctrine about the Bible stands between the Bible and the people so they no longer hear what God speaks through its salvation stories and kingdom teachings. After Josiah's reformation in Judah, the establishment of schools, and the recognition of the authority of the Prophets and Writings along with the Law, there came a fateful day. Now it was thought necessary to declare once and for all which books were to be included in the canon of Scripture (canon meaning "the final rule of faith and practice"). Out of a functional need like this came the attitude we know today as fundamentalism, with its doctrine of biblical infallibility and inerrancy.

This peril leads us to a third corrective method of faith development —*proving*. Proving refers to learning by first-hand encounter with life (not just the classroom). The New Testament Greek language had a word for this, *dokimazo*, which means to prove, to try, to test, as in James 1:2-3, "My brothers and sisters, whenever you face trials of any kind, consider it nothing but joy, because you know that the testing [*dokimion*] of your faith produces endurance; and let endurance have its full effect, so that you may be mature and complete, lacking in nothing."

Jesus taught his disciples primarily through life situations. To be sure he gave them explicit instruction about the kingdom of God, but he was mysteriously secretive about his own divine role in inaugurating the kingdom. The explanation of this so-called messianic secret is to be found in Jesus' admonition, "Do you have eyes, and fail to see? Do you have ears, and fail to hear?" (Mark 8:18).

Part of the Mennonite ethos has always been the priority of life and ethics over doctrine and belief. The fruits of life as proved by love of neighbor and even love of enemy (Matt. 5:43-47) are a better way to know the truth of Christ's teachings than reason or intellectual assent. As the early Anabaptist Hans Denk put it, "No one may truly know Christ except one who follows him in life" (ME, II, 33).

But proving also has its down side. Some Christian educators have so exalted the importance of proving as to make it the primary criterion by which the gospel is known and appropriated. This is the philosophy of *pragmatism*, which asserts that to determine the meaning of any idea, put it into practice in the objective world of actualities. Then whatever the consequences prove to be will constitute the meaning of the idea.

The writings of William C. Bower are especially prone to Christian pragmatism. According to Bower, Jesus began his ministry not with formulated beliefs about who he was but with living persons. Jesus simply began with people's experience of life, seeking to elicit from them a certain "quality of life" that would bless them. "Rather than give them ready-made solutions, Jesus threw people back upon their own resources" (Bower, 23-4). Bower believed that the early church obscured the true image of Jesus as a great moral teacher by deifying him.

Other studies by biblical theologians have shown more clearly that the sense of mission Bower attributed to the early church was not invented by the apostles but given by the deliberate intention of Jesus. So it is much less credible today to picture Jesus as merely going about sharing a pragmatic "quality of life." We can validly see him as one who had received a messianic destiny and proclaimed himself and his church God's chosen agents for the redemption of humanity.

Thus as Christians we both confess that Jesus Christ is the preeminent authority for faith and life and commit ourselves to follow him even when the proof is thin. We also admit that the gospel doesn't always work in the human pragmatic sense. It didn't work for Jesus at Gethsemane and it won't always work for us, *except in the ultimate sphere of the heavenly kingdom.*

This leads, finally, to a fourth conception of faith development—*discipleship.* Discipleship integrates nurture, instruction, and proving. The word disciple means *learner.* Discipleship refers to a direct personal relationship with Jesus Christ as Lord in the midst of his church through which one learns how to live daily in Christ's eternal kingdom (Matt. 11:29).

The faith development processes of nurture, instruction, and proving may not always lead to discipleship, but discipleship always incorporates the other three. Certainly discipleship includes *nurture*—of our children and of ourselves in the fellowship of the church. The first image of discipleship we get from the New Testament is the picture of Jesus in the midst of his followers, including their children. Here the context for nurture was no longer the nuclear human family but the extended "family" of disciples (Mark 3:33-35).

Discipleship also includes the method of continuing *instruction,* not just of our children but especially of ourselves at those times when we must be taught and retaught concerning the deeper meaning of the kingdom of God.

Then certainly discipleship embraces the method of *proving.* We might attend a workshop on "friendship evangelism" (McPhee), but until we begin to apply its principles to our life situations, we will surely fail the ultimate test. We know evangelism belongs to the essential being of the church, yet most of us try to do this work by proxy rather than by our own direct participation. Our conservative church-type representative, Glenn Klassen, spoke to this question in our conversation.

Since my wife started working, I often get my lunch in Hastings. One guy came over and sat down by me at the counter. He didn't know me and I didn't know him, but he spoke with a Low German accent.

I asked him, "What church do you go to?"

He said, "Baptist."

Then he asked me, and I said, "Mennonite."

Next I asked him, "When did you become a Baptist?"

And he said, "I'm not really, but you never tell people in this town that you're a Mennonite."

It's the conscientious objector thing that has given Mennonites a bad name in Hastings, and I said to him, "If you're ashamed of being a Mennonite and all we stand for, maybe you should transfer your membership."

He said he hadn't gone to church for years and confessed to having a drinking problem. "I'm an alcoholic," he said. "Don't ever do what I did, start drinking. It's a terrible life."

I met him there often after that, and we became friends. He came out to the house one Saturday and stayed for night. After breakfast, we went to church together, then I didn't see him for a while.

I got in touch with him at his house, and I said to him, "You were raised in a Mennonite home just like I was. Why don't you ask Christ to save you and then come over and help us to know how to witness to others like yourself?"

He asked me to pray for him, and I told him to pray for himself, and I would listen. About all he could pray was, "Lord, I'll swap my bottle of booze for your peace of mind," but something changed in him right then and there. He started coming to church and didn't hesitate to tell others in our class about his change of heart.

In his testimony before he was baptized, he said, "I've come home at last, and it sure feels good." With that experience something also changed in me, because I hadn't ever led anyone to Christ before. My own faith took on a whole new meaning.

Churches need a "curriculum" in which the method of proving emerges anew as an application of nurture and instruction. An adult Sunday school class whose objective is to learn how to witness would meet each Sunday not only to study a book about it but also to share and review the experiences members had in their attempts to witness during the week.

Summary and Conclusion

In this chapter we reviewed a recent study of the question, "How is faith developed and integrated?" In a survey of 11,122 members of 561 churches from six mainline Protestant denominations, the Search Institute found that about one-third had a mature integrated faith, one-third had an underdeveloped faith, and one-third had an undeveloped faith.

Although we could not make exactly the same evaluation of CMP members, we used some roughly comparable indicators to discover that while Mennonites and Brethren in Christ score substantially higher as a whole, the members of the separatist, conservative, and liberal churches have not as a whole integrated the vertical and horizontal dimensions of faith. Only the members of the transformist churches could be said to have achieved something of a balance between these two dimensions.

We also looked at four methods of faith development—nurture, instruction, proving, and discipleship. The first three are valid processes of religious formation but become corrupted when used alone because they are not inherently grounded in the fullness of Christ (Eph. 4:13). Discipleship is also a process, but it is more than a process. It is grounded in the fullness of Christ in a way that the other three are not, because it alone requires a personal relationship to Christ, the Word of God made flesh (John 1:1). Thus discipleship is both a process of faith development and a criterion by which we test whether any other educational process is authentically Christian. Discipleship is both a means and outcome of faith formation.

Although there are similarities between these four methods of faith development and Westerhoff's four styles of faith (experienced, affiliative, searching, and owned), there are important differences. One is that while Westerhoff refers often to Jesus Christ and the call to be part of a radical community of change agents in the world, he does not speak of discipleship as a faith development process.

Another qualification is that he limits the process of proving, or what he calls "searching," to the teen and early adult years. He does not address an ongoing discernment process in which Christians constantly question whether or not the alternative to what we think is true and right might in fact be true and right, a process calling us in a radically new and different direction as the discerning people of God.

Discussion Questions

1. How would you explain the finding that members of Mennonite and Brethren in Christ churches as a whole scored significantly higher on nineteen questions of faith maturity than members of mainline Protestant churches?

2. Nevertheless, how would you explain the fact that the members of three of the four types of Mennonite/BIC churches as a whole still have underdeveloped faiths—that is, score low either on the vertical or the horizontal dimension of faith?

3. How would you explain the finding that the members of the transformist-type of church as a whole have a more mature faith than the members of the other three types?

4. Should the experience of doubt in the Christian faith, especially by young adults, be accepted and encouraged or rejected and discouraged?

5. What are the strengths and weaknesses of a nurture model of Christian education? Of an instructional model? Of a proving model? Do you see any problems with the discipleship model as defined in this chapter? How does the model of Christian education as discipleship seek to integrate nurture, instruction, and proving into a mature faith?

CHAPTER 7

Who Are We and What Should We Believe?

But how are they to call on one in whom they have not believed?
And how are they to believe in one of whom they have never heard?
—Romans 10:14

PAUL IS SAYING to the Christians in Rome that the Jews (and by implication we could say the Mennonites and Brethren in Christ) have only themselves to blame if they are unclear about who they are or what they should believe. Is it because they have never heard, or because no preacher has been sent to them? The questions are editorial and the implied answers are negative.

The first part of the question asked in the title of this chapter is basic to the theme of our book about the discerning people of God. All of us find ourselves in some social context shared with others. How shall we identify ourselves within this context? Unless we can identify ourselves, we cannot tell ourselves or others who we are and why we think and act as we do.

Among Mennonites the question is read very differently by birthright members and those who joined from other backgrounds. Those who have grown up Mennonite more or less assume that they know what that means, if indeed they have ever seriously asked the question. When outsiders join their church, the question "Who are the Mennonites?" suddenly needs clarification, and church leaders write tracts trying to explain. Such tracts are as illuminating to the natives as to the newcomers, for they usually expose the two facets of Mennonite identity—the ethnic and the religious.

Lois Barrett, who grew up in the Disciples of Christ, joined the Mennonite church because of its peace ethic and caring community. About the latter she candidly wrote,

I have to admit that sometimes the Mennonite sense of community was exclusive, rather than inclusive. In those early years of being a Mennonite, I was working as associate editor of *The Mennonite* at the General Conference offices in Newton, Kansas. As I traveled around the continent to various Mennonite conferences, I met many people who did not know any of my relatives. One woman at a conference told me, upon learning that my husband had grown up Mennonite and I had not, "That's all right, honey. We have a lot of mixed marriages in our congregation, too, and those are fine people."

I have struggled to keep my composure when people asked me if "Barrett," my maiden name, was a Mennonite name. I have kindly told them, "It is now."

The people whose Mennonite identity is connected with *zwieback* and shoofly pie keep reminding me how varied is Mennonite community. It is people who call themselves Mennonite because that is their cultural background, but never attend a Mennonite church. It is people whose biological heritage is Mennonite, but whose theological heritage is fundamentalist or evangelical or liberal. It is people who find their spiritual ancestors in the sixteenth-century Anabaptists. It is people who find in Mennonites a community that keeps pushing the boundaries of what it means to be faithful to the gospel of Christ. It is people who embody a part of a radical perspective on the gospel, and from that perspective bring to birth a new ethnicity, a new sense of peoplehood not based on genealogy. (Barrett, 21-22)

Barrett's reference to a new ethnicity indicates that it is difficult to draw a clear line between the theological and cultural dimensions of the people of God. Culture refers to the sum total of a people's way of doing things, including their way of being faithful to their God. For Christians faith has priority over culture, although even this is blurred for children who grew up Mennonite-Christian and never knew themselves to be anything else. That is why Mennonites stress commitment and believers baptism when children reach the so-called age of accountability. When that rite of passage works according to Anabaptist theology, we can affirm Walter Unger's profession of faith.

For me, being a Mennonite is a way of following Christ and being Christian. . . . I am captivated by that vision of a believers' church of reborn people living reordered lives based on kingdom principles; a vision of corporate discipleship, peacemaking, and a sense of mission which is wholistic—melding word and deed. . . .

For me, being a Mennonite is *not* an ethnic matter, nor is culture the glue which bonds me to this body of believers. Living faith, not ethnicity or culture, defines a Mennonite Christian. (Unger, 297)

Perhaps Unger professes a little too much when he says that "being a Mennonite is not an ethnic matter." John Redekop is nearer the truth when he writes that "whatever the word Mennonite may mean for those of us who are Mennonite by birth as well as rebirth, in our time and in our society it has become primarily an ethnic designation" (Redekop, E, 216). He documents this in many ways, such as listing the number of public agencies in Canada that consider Mennonites to be just one of the numerous ethnic groups rather than a purely religious group. Based on Redekop's analysis, we can define three categories of North American Mennonites.

> 1. *Ethnic Mennonites*, persons who have abandoned religious commitment but are still seen by themselves or others as Mennonites because of their ethnic traits or origins.
> 2. *Ethnic-religious Mennonites*, persons who share the ethnic traits of the first category but are also religiously committed.
> 3. *Religious Mennonites*, persons of non-Mennonite background who have committed themselves to Anabaptist Christianity. Like Lois Barrett, above, they become members of Mennonite churches while denying that they are Mennonites in the ethnic sense of the word. (Redekop, E, 223)

Redekop locates himself within the second category, but he feels that he can do so only by separating the two identities conceptually and giving them different names. He prefers the religious name "Anabaptist." He recommends that the name "Mennonite" be dropped from our church structures and theology and used only to designate our ethnicity. Whether or not this is the best solution to the ongoing dilemma of Mennonite identity deserves further discernment in the church.

As revealed in the following interview excerpts, all four of our representative church members were ethnic-religious Mennonites.

> *Sally Mae Stauffer, separatist.* We were born and raised Old Mennonite. We've been part of Maple Creek church all our lives and our children were brought up here. We've been to other churches when we go along with them and their children, but it's not like the Mennonite Church. It lacks the fellowship we have here.
> *Glenn Klassen, conservative.* I get a lot of satisfaction from my Mennonite roots, but I certainly don't want to be known in town as one who goes around boasting, "I'm a Mennonite." It's far more important to me to be known as a Christian. I learned this from my dad. He lived during the time when they changed from the German to the English, and he was always accused as the one who brought in the English. He taught young married people and pushed English because that was the language they were speaking. He used to say that if our church is going to have any evangelistic outreach in town, we have to learn to speak the language of our English neighbors.
> *Denise Preheim, liberal.* I've traveled all over the country and have never felt any stigma in telling anyone I'm Mennonite. Most people I meet know about Mennonites, and I often cannot believe the good impression they have. Of course a few of them think we're Amish and don't use electricity, but I'm proud of the Mennonite name.
> I do think that when we play the "Mennonite game" of ethnic names and family relationships we sometimes have a problem assimilating people

who join from other backgrounds. Our congregation is still 90% ethnic Mennonite, and it is up to us to put first things first and to be just as interested in their names and family backgrounds.

Menno Isaac, transformist. I would rather be identified as Anabaptist than as Mennonite. In a large urban center like Hamilton, people still think of Mennonites as the horse-and-buggy people they see around Waterloo. At work I do not hesitate to say that I'm a Mennonite pacifist, but in dealing with my fellow engineers it's more important to state clearly why I believe that warfare and militarism are wrong.

Gauging Ethnic Identity

Now we turn to specific ways ethnic and religious identity were measured in the Church Member Profile research project and how our measurements correlated with our types of Mennonite and Brethren in Christ congregations.

We begin with a preliminary probe of emotional attachments to the name Mennonite (or Brethren in Christ). The majority of members in all four church types do not want their churches to drop the name, even though many cannot say that they get "very much" or "a great deal" of satisfaction at being known by this name "in the eyes of other people."

Readers may be surprised to hear that liberal-type church members respond more positively to the two Mennonite identity indicators—"gets satisfaction from being known as Mennonite or Brethren in Christ" and "does not want the congregation to drop the name"—than members of the other three church types. Apparently the name is well enough known in the larger social context that nearly two-thirds of the liberal members, who would probably reject a separatist or conservative identity, feel good about being publicly identified as Mennonite.

These indicators, of course, do not reveal whether that identity is primarily ethnic or religious. For the more specifically ethnic profile, we asked respondents a series of ten questions about the extent to which they identified with ingroup Mennonite (BIC) family, friends, language, schools, and organizations. Again readers may be surprised to find that members of the liberal and transformist church types scored higher on the composite ethnicity index than members of the two conservative types. This was due mainly to their favorable attitudes toward promoting in-group schools, learning the ethnic language, and supporting in-group organizations. Separatist members scored noticeably higher on the more socially restrictive elements of the scale—in-group marriage, in-group dating and in-group friends.

When gauged by all of these probes, it is evident that ethnicity has several distinct factors—social restrictiveness in a separatist community, and in-group education for a Mennonite way of life that is not necessarily separatist or conservative. In further discernment of pros and cons of Mennonite ethnicity versus a more explicitly religious identity, we will try to sort out these factors.

Gauging Religious Identity

Members who grow up in Mennonite/BIC homes often have little sense of the difference between their ethnic and their religious identity until they reach an age of faith maturation. At that stage (as portrayed in the previous chapter) it becomes more crucial for young adults to ponder historical and theological roots. Then they become more aware that faith also has multiple facets—integrating belief and behavior, experience and practice, conversion and baptism, knowledge and commitment, worship and service, congregational and denominational identity, congregational involvement and individualistic expressions of faith.

The faith maturation process can be thwarted at any stage by the absence or dominance of any one of these developmental elements. As Walter Klaassen put it, "The labels we use to identify ourselves, including the denominational ones, are like fig leaves that cover only part of us. They are insufficient to cover all that one is. They have their utility, but they cannot pass for a suit of clothes" (Klaassen, C, 146).

In our church member research project, the percentage profiles of our four types of congregation were compared by considering six kinds of religious identity.

1. *Congregational Identity*. One of the best known marks of being Mennonite or BIC is attending a Mennonite or BIC congregation. From the beginning of Anabaptist-Mennonite history, these people have been gathering into congregations. "They believed that the church should be a visible gathering of true believers, that it should be voluntary, and that it should be a community in which the totality of life is shared and regulated for the glory of God and the highest good of humankind" (Kauffman/Harder, 64).

There is always a price to be paid for this corporate covenantal mark of peoplehood. It is remarkable that the majority of the members seem willing to pay that price—the sacrifice of certain degrees of individual freedom so members can be and do together what no one can be and do alone. However, for a variety of reasons some persons with a former Mennonite identity have abandoned the congregational obligation, preferring to live their lives more or less without these corporate constraints. Nor can it be said that every remaining member is equally or fully involved. The percentage of members who attend Sunday worship regularly varies from 49% in liberal congregations to 74% in separatist congregations.

2. *Denominational Identity*. The liberal congregations, which measured lowest on congregational involvement, measured highest for denominational identity. For members of liberal churches, the denomination satisfies certain needs that are not the same as those satisfied by congregational involvement alone. Liberals apparently feel that there are some things that congregations must do together to fulfill their mission in the world.

The separatist churches, on the other hand, are often critical of denominational leadership for being too centralized and spendthrift. They prefer to invest more of their resources and interest in the local congregation where they have more control.

3. *General Orthodoxy*. Mennonites and Brethren in Christ have always had fervent convictions which they believe to be based on the life and teachings of Christ. They have generally placed more emphasis on living the faith than on believing it, at least when believing was defined as intellectual assent as distinct from to the commitment of one's life to the lordship of Christ. As the preamble to the 1963 Mennonite Confession of Faith put it, "In its beliefs the Mennonite Church is bound ultimately to the Holy Scriptures, not to any human formulation of doctrine" (MCF, 45). Or as Menno Simons put it, "The Scriptures do not need interpretation; they need to be obeyed" (Howard Loewen, 16).

The wellspring of Mennonite beliefs was not some sixteenth-century theological system but the ancient creeds of the one holy apostolic church. The doctrinal differences between sixteenth-century Anabaptist leaders and other Christians pertained not as much to core beliefs as to the degree of seriousness with which they felt the beliefs should be applied to daily living (Kauffman/Harder, 102).

As a gauge of adherence to general Christian beliefs, six items from a national interdenominational study were used. In comparisons to the responses of other denominational groups, Mennonites and Brethren in Christ members are near the top of the doctrinal orthodoxy scale. While all four of our congregational types scored substantially higher than did Protestants as a whole, the responses of our liberal members were significantly less orthodox than those of the other three church types.

These differences should not be threatening so long as there is freedom in the churches to discuss them and in so doing to rethink traditional doctrine in the light of discipleship. Some will look for guidelines in the Anabaptist witness. Others will be wary of Anabaptist doctrine because they resist its emphasis on a discipleship lifestyle and peace witness. The future discernment of beliefs may well bring the older tensions between fundamentalism and liberalism to the surface again unless some new perspectives are found to guide the discussion. It will help to remember that for Menno Simons and the Anabaptists, traditional doctrine was secondary to discipleship.

4. *Fundamentalist Identity.* Fundamentalism refers to a twentieth-century reaction within North American Protestantism to what its advocates consider corrosive tendencies to let science and culture corrupt biblical theology . For instance, the theory of evolution challenged the traditional biblical doctrine of creation and prompted reinterpretation of the Genesis account. So-called modernism, on the other side, "was the banning of God from the creation of the universe and thereby implicitly from his continuing role in the world" (P. Toews, 318).

Fundamentalism was organized to purge modernism from various Protestant denominations. Checklists of six or more so-called fundamentals were used as tests of orthodoxy. Fundamentals included the inerrancy of the Bible, the creation of the universe in six days according to Genesis, the substitutionary atonement of Christ, the bodily resurrection of Christ, the future premillenial return of Christ, and the future judgment of all people dividing those saved from those lost to everlasting punishment. Some who accepted these beliefs did not hesitate to condemn those who questioned them. Thus the fundamentals were valued not only for their content but also as a tool to exclude modernists from positions of leadership or even membership.

North American fundamentalism had an impact on Mennonites in both respects—the content of the checklists and their use in efforts to purge the churches of modernism. In the Mennonite Church (MC), Goshen College was closed for a year so a number of teachers could be dismissed and the school reorganized "to be more in harmony with the conservative stand of the church" (Grant Stoltzfus, 24). The MC denomination adopted a new confession of faith called "The Christian Fundamentals" in order "to give expression to some of the doctrines and practices of the early church which at that time were not a matter of difference, but have since . . . been questioned or denied by many church organizations" (Howard Loewen, 71).

About one-eighth of the more liberal minded members of the Indiana-Michigan Conference (MC) formed new congregations that joined the more progressive General Conference Mennonite Church (GCMC), which subsequently endured its own doctrinal controversies. The Mennonite Brethren Church (MBC), Evangelical Mennonite Church (EMC), and Brethren in Christ (BIC) avoided some of this controversy by aligning themselves with conservative evangelical groups early on, such as the National Association of Evangelicals (the moderate wing of the fundamentalist movement). In so doing, these otherwise peace churches have been less than fully aware how nationalism and civil religion began to undermine their Anabaptist ethic of nonresistance. As Yoder put it, "What is the use of having a checklist requiring people to accept the biblical view of the cross of Christ if that acceptance does not issue in a biblical view of the cross of the Christian?" (Yoder, A, 39-40).

In our 1975 CMP I book, *Anabaptists Four Centuries Later*, we claimed that the fundamentalist movement had largely spent itself. In review, C. Norman Kraus wrote that "quite the opposite has happened. Fundamentalism has recouped, reorganized, and clearly defined itself as a movement over against evangelicalism. . . . The distinctive characteristics of this new fundamentalism are biblical literalism and inerrancy, rightist political convictions and activity, and the championing of a 'Christian America' " (Kraus, 36-37, 40).

To gauge the extent of commitment to fundamentalism in our groups, a fundamentalist beliefs index was constructed, comprising some of the main items on the checklist. We discovered that among members of the four types of churches, fundamentalism is more a function of the conservative-liberal factor than of the separationist-integrationist factor. The six-day creation doctrine is not held as strongly as the other doctrines listed, but support for the idea of using these fundamentals as a test of membership is over 80% in every church type except liberal (68%). Fundamentalism as a belief system appears still to be entrenched, especially in the separatist churches, despite their alleged separation from the world.

5. *Anabaptist Identity*. We turn finally to the dimension of religious belief that most explicitly defines the normative identity of Mennonites and Brethren in Christ—Anabaptism. In the 1972 CMP I research project, H. S. Bender's influential address, "The Anabaptist Vision," was used as the theological definition of Anabaptism (Kauffman/Harder, 114ff.). While recognizing the "mosaic of groupings of [Anabaptist] dissenters," Walter Klaassen more recently listed three themes "held in common following the crystallization of the movement between 1527 and 1540."

> 1. All shared a view of salvation as human and divine cooperation. Justification was seen as progression in holiness; the ethic of the Sermon on the Mount was the guide to it.
> 2. Baptism [of believers] was considered to be the sign of lay emancipation from clerical control and the spiritual enfranchisement of lay people (priesthood of all believers).
> 3. Anabaptists developed a communal Christianity centered on the congregation, in contrast to the clericalized territorial churches, both Catholic and Protestant. (Klaassen, D, 24)

In view of Klaassen's assent to Anabaptist diversity and disavowal of Bender's normative vision as "too tidy, too ideal," it is amazing how similar the two summaries are.

To gauge adherence to Anabaptist beliefs for CMP I and CMP II, we wrote a number of questions based on the common elements in the statements of Bender and Klaassen. These elements are discipleship as the essence of Christian being, the congregation of believers as the essence of the church, and the practice of love and nonresistance as the essence of Christian ethics. We discovered that members of the transformist churches, who scored lowest on the fundamentalism scale, ranked highest on the Anabaptism index. Conversely, the conservative churches that scored second highest on fundamentalism scored lowest on Anabaptism.

Anabaptist Vision and Mennonite Reality

Five kinds of religious identity of members of Mennonite and Brethren in Christ types of churches were gauged in the preceding paragraphs as a strong counterpoint to the ethnic identity measured earlier in the chapter. It seems that our people as a whole have a broad repertoire of religious and cultural expressions, but are they being integrated around a common core of Anabaptist beliefs?

Scholars have not agreed in their assessments. On one hand, Bender believed that "American Mennonitism on the whole is still sound at the core, has to a large extent recovered its sense of connection with its great past, has developed a large capacity for self criticism. . . , and has a good balance of faith and works." Bender believed that a revitalized church would reject fundamentalism and find its central identity in Anabaptist history and theology, for here we find the balance between the gospel of salvation and a Christian social conscience and responsibility "which was strangely absent from fundamentalism" (H. Bender, A, 47).

On the other side, Yoder concluded that the Anabaptist vision and Mennonite reality are in serious discontinuity and in certain ways incompatible.

> So what we have is not an Anabaptist community when measured by the criteria which we have stated. It is rather a small *Christendom*. . . . Mennonitism still finds its identity most properly on the ethnic community level. . . . Precisely because the language of Anabaptism has so long been used as a reinforcement of Mennonite self-confidence, the Mennonite population is now refractory beyond the average to the Anabaptist message, having been, as it were, vaccinated. Mennonites are less avid in asking to see the novelty of the Anabaptist witness than are Christians of other kinds of backgrounds. This is no reproach; they are struggling to overcome a conception of their inherited distinctness and separateness which is neither biblical nor viable in the modern world or the modern church. But what we are trying to test now is not whether this observation gives reason to scold someone. The question is whether it is into the root stock of the heirs of Mennonite culture that God is most likely to be able to engraft the new radi-

cal reformation reality which is his will for the modern world. (Yoder, F, 6, 34, 40)

With these assessments in the background, we can bring this chapter to a climax by testing the truth of the matter with the church member data. We examined the correlations between five of our identity factors (ethnic identity, congregational identity, general orthodoxy, fundamentalism, and Anabaptism) and four ethical indicators (peace witness, welfare attitudes, race relations, and support for the worldwide ministries of the Mennonite Central Committee). We discovered that fundamentalist identity has the greatest magnitude of influence, but that the influence in every case is negative. The more fundamentalist a member is, the *less* he or she tends to support peace witness, social welfare, race relations, and the work of MCC.

The average intercorrelation of Anabaptist identity, second in rank, is not quite as great, but the direction of its relationships is positive for all four ethical indicators. The correlations were far from perfect and Anabaptism also has some negative correlations (such as political involvement, interchurch relations, and women in church leadership), but as a whole Anabaptist identity seems to have an overall wholesome influence on our members, moving them toward social ethical responsibility in areas like racism, poverty, war, and international conflict.

Concluding Comments

Mennonites and Brethren in Christ have been and remain a reflective people, with resources in their congregations and conferences to review these assessments and to discern what they should believe concerning them. It is hoped that they will ask serious questions about where they have come from, what they believe, and why there seems to be some contradiction between a fundamentalist and an Anabaptist orientation. Then under guidance of the Advocate they will take up anew their mandate from Christ to reconsider the ground of their peoplehood and the content of their beliefs. Harold Bender inspired us by the vision he portrayed of our roots in the radical reformation, but we now have to revise the parts that were "too tidy, too ideal," to repeat Walter Klaassen's admonition.

We also need to hear the true stories about early Anabaptist leaders like Conrad Grebel, Michael Sattler, Balthasar Hubmaier, Melchior Hoffman, David Joris, Menno Simons, Pilgram Marpeck, and Hans Denk, for while they all had a part of the truth, none had the whole truth. Denk thought it was important to wrestle with paradoxes in the Scriptures, such as the one that contrasts "I will not be angry forever" (Jer. 3:12) and

"These will go away into eternal punishment" (Matt. 25:46). Denk declared that "two opposing Scripture passages must both be true. One will be contained in the other as the lesser in the greater, as time in eternity, finitude in infinity. He who gives up on opposing Scripture passages and cannot find their unity lacks the ground of truth" (Moore, 146).

There are many Anabaptist stories we have yet to hear. Once we have heard them, we can claim them as our own, not because they are "tidy and ideal," but because they represent the struggle to discern the truth together about the call into Christ's kingdom and the courage to ask again and again, "Who are we and what should we believe?"

Discussion Questions

1. How would you answer the question, "Who are the Mennonites?" (or "Who are the Brethren in Christ?") for someone who asks? Discuss different ways the question can be answered.

2. Can there be any Christianity free of an ethnic or cultural dimension?

3. Should the name "Mennonite" be dropped from our church structures and theologies? Would "Anabaptist" be preferable? Or "Evangelical"?

4. Why do you think the members of liberal-type churches tend to score highest of the four church types on Mennonite identity? Why do the members of conservative-type churches tend to score lowest on ethnic identity? Why do the members of separatist-type churches tend to score highest on congregational identity? Why do the members of transformist-type churches tend to score highest on Anabaptist identity?

5. Are there positive things to be said about fundamentalism?

6. What are the positive and negative things to be said about Anabaptism? Can we find a positive identity in Anabaptism without making it "too tidy, too ideal," to use Walter Klaassen's admonition?

CHAPTER 8

Can We Be Faithful Without Joining the Church?

The man from whom the demons had gone begged that he might be with him;
but Jesus sent him away, saying, "Return to your home,
and declare how much God has done for you."
—Luke 8:38-39

THE MAN WANTED TO JOIN the company of disciples, but Jesus sent him home. In this chapter we face another question for discernment concerning the tensions between individualism and community in the Christian life. We can certainly begin with the premise that a person is both an individual and a member of multiple groups and that neither dimension exhausts the reality of personhood. If individualism considers only a part of the person, collectivism considers the person only as a part of a group.

As we prepared to update the 1972 Church Member Profile, we heard from pastors and denominational leaders that a growing problem for the church today is individualism, the attitude that Christians can be faithful without getting involved in the church. From their experience, individualism is the attitude of the church member who when visited by the stewardship committee to make a pledge to the church budget replied, "I don't believe in pledging. I can go into my closet as Jesus taught and pray to my God free of charge!"

This comment illustrates a trend toward what Robert Bellah and his associates described as pathological individualism. We can benefit from their insights in distinguishing between wholesome and unwholesome individualism.

Types of Individualism

In 1985 Robert Bellah and four coauthors published their best-selling book, *Habits of the Heart*, a sociological interpretation of individualism and communal commitment that was read and discussed in many adult Sunday school classes across North America. The authors defined individualism in two contrasting senses (Bellah *et al.*, 334).

Wholesome Individualism	Unwholesome Individualism
1. Biblical Individualism	1. Utilitarian Individualism
2. Civic Individualism	2. Expressive Individualism

In the first category, the community is as vital as its individual members; both are seen as creations of God. In utilitarian and expressive individualism, community is formed, if at all, for what the members can get out of it for themselves.

Biblical Individualism. The Scriptures speak often about the priceless value and merit of every person. Jesus taught that "even the hairs of your head are all counted. So do not be afraid; you are of more value than many sparrows" (Matt. 10:30). It follows that for a person to exchange wholesome for unwholesome individuality is a calamity, "for what will it profit them if they gain the whole world but forfeit their life?" (Matt. 16:26).

Mennonites and Brethren in Christ have tried to keep their traditional communalism in proper balance with a biblical individualism, although not always successfully. Sometimes the community has smothered individuality, and sometimes individualism has undermined community. But in principle, according to the Anabaptist vision, "the greatest degree of liberty must be granted the individual conscience in spiritual matters, [for] Anabaptism was the essence of individualism" (Smith, 21).

Civic Individualism. In this second type, concern for others is expressed in participation in the civic affairs of the community. In Mennonite history, civic individualism has taken the form of living in separated agricultural communities. There were towns and villages across Canada and the United States in which much of the population was Mennonite. They were called Mennonite communities because they maintained enough geographic isolation "to give the community sufficient autonomy to qualify as 'religious' community and to embody a 'unique way of life' " (J. L. Burkholder, A, 100-1).

Under the impact of social change, these forms of rural community are now largely extinct, but the tradition of civic individualism survives in other forms. Mennonites have increasingly felt led to make known in their communities and the wider society their concerns about such issues as war and peace, temperance, and economic reform (Juhnke, B).

Utilitarian Individualism. In contrast to the first two types, utilitarian and expressive individualism focus on the self as the primary reality and fashion a style of life that is inherently unwholesome. Utilitarianism is a form of individualism devoted to the calculating pursuit of one's own material interest (Bellah, 336).

Bellah and associates interpret the so-called American dream as promoting utilitarian individualism by promising everyone the opportunity to succeed economically by individual initiative when in fact the dream often promises more than it can deliver. Then people resort to all kinds of immoral behavior to get the jump on competitors and force the dream to come true.

The reader will recall the interview with Glenn Klassen in chapter 1. Glenn talked about his Mennonite neighbor who plugged his drainage tile and flooded his rented land because the neighbor had wanted to rent that land for himself. Under the stress of competition, he resorted to an immoral utilitarian tactic.

The history of Mennonites in the North American free enterprise environment is the story of constant tension between their biblical-civic traditions and pressures to become utilitarian individualists in the material realm (Nafziger, 187-204). Their discipleship ethic sets strict limits on a self-serving approach to economic endeavor. Work is supposed to be worthwhile in itself and not merely a means to get ahead financially.

But industry produces prosperity, prosperity results in wealth, and wealth introduces a dilemma for a people whose ethic disapproves of materialistic self-interest and conspicuous consumption. As our people entered the work places of modern commerce and industry, they began to compromise their ethic and substitute traits of utilitarian individualism—economic shrewdness and indiscriminate use of commercial law.

Expressive Individualism. The fourth type arose out of the culture of modern psychotherapy as a treatment for the emotional disturbances caused by the dilemmas of utilitarianism. Through many forms of psychotherapy, people abused in the free enterprise system discover an alternative promise of happiness in the pursuit of self-development and self-actualization (Bellah, 333-4). In the end, this type also fails to serve the deeper interests of both individual and community because it is inherently self-centered and perpetuates an infantile stage of human development in which throughout life the self is the chief object of a person's interest.

Urban Mennonite and Brethren in Christ churches are especially vulnerable to the temptations of expressive individualism. The urban Mennonite congregation studied in depth by sociologist Joseph Smucker "looks very little like the 'ethical community' of biblical individualism and much more like a sort of 'pit stop for emotional refueling and identity reinforcement' " (Ainley, 146-7; J. Smucker, 273-91).

Gauging Mennonite Individualism

In the CMP II research project, an attempt was made to measure the degree to which members of our five denominations could be characterized by the Bellah types of individualism. Overall, 69% of our CMP respondents are very committed to "being at peace with other persons," 61% believe it is very important to treat others properly, and 23% that it is important to use one's personal resources for the good of others—all indicators of biblical individualism.

On our indicators of civic individualism, 76% frequently or occasionally do voluntary work for the church or community agencies, 74% agree that members should witness directly to the state or nation by writing to legislators, 71% favor having an office in our national capitols to communicate the ethical concerns of our Mennonite Central Committee, and 64% voted in all or most elections in recent years.

On the materialistic side of individualism, 33% say it is important to work hard to get ahead financially, 19% to earn as much money as possible, 8% to get the nicest home and furnishings one can afford, and 7% to be dressed in the latest styles and fashions.

On indicators of expressive individualism, 34% say "being free to do what I want to do" is important and 32% that the pursuit of pleasure is a valid way to keep some balance and enjoyment in life. But only 3% say the phrase "if it feels good, do it" is a good principle of life for the Christian today.

Comparing the percentages for the first two individualism types, we observe first that among Mennonites and BICs, the members of separatist churches tend to score highest on biblical individualism. Members of liberal churches scored highest on civic individualism. The transformist churches appear most successful in integrating both forms of wholesome individualism.

The percentages for the more unwholesome forms of individualism reveal another profile. The members of conservative churches tend to score highest on utilitarian individualism, and the members of liberal churches score highest on expressive individualism.

The overall picture suggests that while the biblical and civic traditions are still intact, with over half of the members of all four types of congregations affirming a self-for-others ethic, these traditions are being threatened by utilitarian and expressive individualism. Certainly there is potential tension in our churches between the pathological forms of individualism and commitment to the social welfare of others.

The Perennial Call to Church Renewal

Nothing is more constant in the history of the church than the call for church renewal, which is like the rising and receding of the ocean tide. At times renewal recedes into the background and is obscured by many other concerns. Then it rises in importance again, billowing in upon our minds with new force. As these words are being written, the call to church renewal seems to be in recession, but it will surely sweep in upon us again before long.

Toward the end of the first century, the author of the last book of the Bible was writing to the seven churches of Asia Minor, "Remember then from what you have fallen; repent, and do the works you did at first" (Rev. 2:5). Because the Anabaptists had a radical vision for the reformation of the church, Mennonite and BIC congregations have been subjected to severe criticism in every generation, especially by their own disillusioned young adults. Our dropout rates are very high. The reasons are many, but a degree of cynicism characterizes most of our dropouts (Steiner, 91).

Denise Preheim, our representative liberal church member in chapter 1, was a dropout following her graduation from the Mennonite seminary when she was unable to get employment as a pastor or associate pastor. In commenting on her reasons for leaving the church for almost a decade, she said,

> After searching in vain for my niche in the church, I had the scary feeling that there was none. I went to Washington and entered two years of clinical pastoral education, but I had no interest in attending church anywhere, especially not a Mennonite church.
>
> I made new friends in CPE, and most of us were church dropouts. In a sense, we became church to each other in our hospital environment. These people accepted me as a minister, and I found the love and support that I had missed in the Mennonite churches of my past. This realization gave me the permission to leave the church. Over a decade later I returned, when I finally found one in which I could be myself. But I'll probably always be something of a church critic.

In the church renewal literature of a former decade, three major indictments are leveled at the mainline churches and are increasingly applicable to Mennonite and BIC churches today (L. Harder, G, 4-11). One is that the church has become an *establishment* of society. The relationship between North American churches and our national ethos today is often described as "civil religion" (Kraybill, C, 163-5). As a form of civic individualism, this is not inherently unwholesome, but congregations are under great pressure to justify whatever the nation does, especially in times of international conflict and war.

Peter Berger fears that because of its establishment in American society, the church has rendered itself unable or unwilling to stand against the pressures of cultural conformity at many points where principles of Christian ethics are at stake. He believes that the main problem of the church is "the effectiveness with which the religious establishment is designed to prevent the encounter with the Christian message" (Berger, B, 115). Far from picking up its cross and following Christ, the established church ratifies the utilitarian and expressive middle-class values prevalent in society.

A second indictment of the church is its success orientation. The local congregation typically measures the effectiveness of its program by statistical and financial indexes. The construction and maintenance of a modern church building and the support of a trained professional minister require hundreds of thousands of dollars. The image of success that accompanies these commitments requires a sizable membership, a rising budget, and an expanding program. This mindset determines the kind of church planting strategy used by most denominations—a "high potential site" for the new edifice, a respectable architectural design, and a full-time church planting specialist.

The cynics have argued that if the church of today took the New Testament as its model, it would be seen as a failure even as Jesus was seen as a failure. "There is little room in the churches for the person who feels that funds might be better channeled into active programs of service than into the construction of bigger and better church properties. . . . How many new churches decide not to build?. . . . How many churches feel free to experiment, to follow the promptings of the Spirit, to try new ways of service?" (Rose, 9).

A third failure of the church is its insulation from the world, where the main drama of spiritual warfare between Christ and Satan is being waged. When the majority of the people lived in small rural communities, there was a rationale for a residential church serving primarily a local community in which members lived. But today most of us live in cities in which our places of residence and work are separate spheres. The church captive to the sphere of residence has little influence on the sphere of work.

> The residential community in which most pastorates are exercised is no longer the dynamic center of society. Home is the place for licking one's wounds, finding refuge in personal relationships, and enjoying a certain leisure. Residence and family life *react* to the dynamics of society, suffering anxieties that are engendered in the productive process. . . . The strains of industrial production are such that pastors deal with widespread emotional disturbance in these residential communities without access to the sources of these disturbances. They deal with the symptoms: broken home, dis-

turbed personalities, and delinquent children. The load of personal, pastoral care increases day by day, but the forces that create these problems become daily more remote from the pastor in the residential community. The pastor ministers in a sanitarium, treating the shock cases but never discovering the enemy who is inflicting the damage. (Winter, 29)

When we move from the indictments to the remedies, we cannot help being disappointed. Imaginative images of new forms of the church are many, but there are few actual models pointing the way. Three typical remedies are found in the literature of church renewal (L. Harder, G, 11-18).

The first remedy can be described as *rugged individualism*. To Peter Berger this means that "whoever would freely encounter truth must pay the price of being alone" (Berger, B, 120). There is a strong Anabaptist ingredient in this affirmation, with its accent on "the decisive turning point that occurs in the human life as a result of encountering the message of Jesus Christ" (Berger, B, 114), but Berger's disillusionment with the local congregation is so severe that he despairs for its renewal. He believes it has too many vested interests to be able to shake loose from its captivity, and his prescription calls for disengagement.

> Let there be no uncertainty as to what we are saying: we are suggesting that Christians may freely choose *not* to become members of local congregations, *not* to identify themselves with a denomination, *not* to join the weekly traffic jam of the religious rush hour on Sunday morning. We are suggesting that these decisions might be directly grounded in the Christian faith as it seeks to relate itself to our situation. And we are contending that such decisions might be the legitimate exercise of a Christian vocation in our time. (Berger, B, 177)

A whimsical critique of this cop-out was written by Robert McAfee Brown, who tried to imagine what the impact of Berger's attitude would be in the lives of the college students for whom he was writing.

> BERGER READER (having finished page 180 and shut *The Noise of Solemn Assemblies*): Well, thank goodness! I'm off the hook as far as the "church" is concerned. I can be a Christian without being a churchman at all. Let those silly people keep on with their rituals and hymns and communion services and helping individuals in need if they want to. I'm beyond all that. Now that I see how anachronistic it all is, I'm free.
>
> Instead of that I'll . . . I'll. . . . Let's see now, what shall I do? The church can't really change the structures of society and it hasn't got much of a future erecting signs of "Christian presence." I'll have to get into Christian dialogue. But where and how? There isn't any structure around to foster it, and besides, I don't really know the score on the Christian faith. I'll just have to go it alone. But no matter. How nice, how *very* nice, not to have to feel guilty about the church any more. (Brown, 339)

A second response to the impotence of the local congregation can be described with the term in our section heading: *renewal*. This approach focuses on the revival and retooling of the local congregation. *The Parish Paper* edited by Lyle Schaller contains many ideas for the rejuvenation of the congregation, such as the following:

• Ministry should be performed as a partnership between pastor and people with greater involvement of the laity.

• The preaching ministry of the pastor should challenge as well as comfort the people with special appeals for community intervention from time to time.

• The laity should handle many of the administrative tasks so that the pastor is free to concentrate on what he was trained for: preparing sermons, making pastoral calls, counseling persons, and equipping the laity for their discipleship.

• Limited funds should be distributed more equitably between local needs and outreach.

• Fundraising should be limited to a single annual appeal centered in a pledge system.

• More joint services with other churches in the community should be planned.

• Ecumenical youth choirs and other joint programs should be developed.

• Service to the community and the world should be top priority for the church, and no barriers to service should be tolerated once the needs are determined.

• The church building should be open to community needs, and Christians working with lonely people or homeless persons, alcoholics, families of the terminally ill, etc., should be invited to use the church's facilities.

• Congregations should set new goals every year and write statements of covenant to pursue such goals within a time frame.

• The integrity of membership should be evaluated in relation to such a covenant, and an annual covenant renewal should be planned.

• Members ought to view their congregational participation as a calling from God, and congregations should have specific ways to hold members accountable for their pastor-people partnership in the mission of the church.

The third approach to the problem of the church goes beyond renewal to *reformation*. In an article entitled "Not Renewal, But Reformation," Gordon Cosby, well-known pastor of the Church of the Saviour in Washington, D.C., wrote that "when the structures get as rigid and as resistant to change as they are now, perhaps the wisest strategy is not to try to renew them . . . [but to] bypass them and let God do with them what he will. The new structures which will appear may be so drastically different from the old as to constitute reform rather than renewal" (Cosby, 4).

Cosby's thesis is that the shape of the church ought to grow out of its mission and that the structures of the typical congregation do not allow it to be on mission. Even as the new wine of the gospel required new wineskins (Matt. 9:17), radical obedience to Christ always results in new strategies and new structures. As a kind of brainstorming exercise, Cosby presented the following reformation possibilities.

> I think we ought to be open to giving up all professional ministries. It may be that I ought to earn my livelihood another way. Perhaps all of the ministers of a congregation should be engaged in a tent-making ministry and do their job in the life of the world.
>
> Another possibility is that of giving up all real estate. . . . If a bomb were to fall on this area, we would have to be the church without any real estate. The church was the church during the most vibrant period of its life, several hundred years, without real estate.
>
> Another possibility is that the church might carry out its mission through small bands of people, just two or three or four or five, who would live out their lives in the midst of the world of business, the world of government, the world of mass media, the medical world, the educational world—out there where they are making their tents, earning their living. Such little mission groups would be working at the problems of mass media, or on the issues relating to peace and prevention of war, or on race relations and housing, or with the poor, perhaps taking a vow of poverty.
>
> I am not talking about little functional groups related to the local congregation. These mission groups would be the local congregation. We need to redefine the meaning of congregation. "Where two or three are gathered together in my name, there am I in the midst of them" (Matt. 18:20). This is the beginning point. What does it mean to gather—to "congregate"—in the name of Christ? It means to have been baptized into his nature. To have died with him and risen with him. It presupposes commitment. (Cosby, 5-6)

Anyone who applauds the ideas of these dissidents risks presumption at numerous points. The first, as Cosby suggested, is the quality of one's personal commitment to Christ and the church. Much talk about the irrelevance of old forms can be just one more way to evade Christ's call to personal repentance and discipleship. Another is the maturity of one's theology. The rugged individualist approach subverts the doctrine of the church as an essential part of the gospel of Christ (see chapter 2). The renewal approach deals largely with symptoms and bypasses the prior question of commitment. The reformation approach, while more radical, can fail to comprehend that radicals who repudiate the old structures and create new ones will ultimately face the same pressures that corrupted the old ones.

The Essential Conditions for the Church's Existence

It is customary for Christian theologians to define the church in terms of its essential marks. As a climax to this chapter, we will approach our initial question from a socio-biblical perspective. As a group (or movement) of followers of Jesus Christ, the church is certainly more than a merely human group. Yet the church is also undeniably human and faced with the same human factors as any other group. Any group, including the church, requires a set of conditions by which members must interact if they want to work together for shared ends (Greer, 18ff.). With all the risks involved, Jesus took the task in hand and founded the one holy catholic church, made up of willing and wavering members (see Luke 9:57-63) charged with limiting and defining the spread of the heavenly kingdom throughout the world. The churches that Paul helped to plant were certainly comprised of all kinds of people—many of them deeply committed and others obstinate and unruly.

Sociologically there are three essential conditions to be met for a church to have an appropriate group structure. The first condition is *clearly defined purposes and goals*. This has to do with the needs that the church fulfills, its reasons for existing, and its basic objectives. The assumption is that members have to come together to be and do certain things no individual can do alone.

The second condition is *a networking process*. From such networking must evolve a system of roles and a basis of authority to carry out the church's purposes. The members of this church have met Christ and accepted his plan of salvation and call to discipleship. Through discernment of spiritual gifts, some take leadership and others accept the authority of this leadership. In time each member is given tasks to perform in the pursuit of the church's purposes.

The third condition is *disciplined behavior*. Discipline keeps members cooperating when "the spirit . . . is willing but the flesh is weak" (Mark 14:38). Discipline involves creating a minimal accountability structure based on rewards and chastenings (Matt. 18:15-18, John 15:1-2).

In the CMP II questionnaire, items were designed to describe the member's local congregation in relation to the three conditions of church formation. Nine items had to do with condition 1—the purposes and goals of the church.

The four types of churches tend to view their purposes somewhat differently. In the separatist churches, Jesus is seen more as the personal Savior who died for our sins (81%) than as the suffering servant who calls us to follow his example (19%). This contrasts with 61%/39% in the liberal churches. Separatists also feel it is more important to help individuals find a personal saving faith (88%) than to work for a more just and equitable world (12%), contrasted to 52%/48% in the liberal churches. The implicit tension indicated by these contrasting conceptions of the church's primary purpose characterizes churches of all denominations.

In relation to condition 2, strong participation of the membership in "the important congregational decisions" is reported by 82% of our respondents, with no significant differences between our four types of congregation.

But on three attitudinal questions pertaining to role authority, there are significant differences. In the separatist churches there is 22% assent to the participation of women in ministerial leadership, contrasted to 72% of members of liberal churches. Members of transformist churches tend most to affirm the participation of the laity in ministry and a more limited role for set-apart ordained ministers. As a whole, however, 48% of all respondents believe a congregation cannot be complete unless there is an ordained minister to lead the congregation and perform the ministerial functions, and only 67% believe that all members should participate as they are able in the ministerial functions of the church.

In relation to condition 3, the doctrine and practice of church discipline is most in evidence in the separatist churches, 68% of whose members report that in their congregations a member guilty of an attitude or act sinful by the church's standard is normally confronted and counseled to repent. In the liberal churches, the corresponding percentage is 22 points lower—perhaps an indication of some resistance to the traditional Mennonite and BIC practice of church discipline. The issue of an alternative way to work at membership accountability needs new study and discernment in our congregations.

Summary and Conclusion

In the perspective of biblical theology, individualism has both a positive and negative side. On the plus side, there are many references in the Bible to the sacredness and worth of each person, created in the image of God and redeemed at great cost. In this chapter, this was discussed as "biblical individualism." Part of God's redemption is the community grounded in a covenant between God and his people. This was discussed as "civic individualism." Mennonites and Brethren in Christ have strong biblical and civic traditions.

On the minus side, there are forces in modern life that make people competitive, materialistic, self-centered, and uncaring for the needs of others. This was described in two categories of unwholesome individualism—"utilitarian" and "expressive." Like most church groups, Mennonites and Brethren in Christ are caught up in the process of becoming more modern and individualistic at the expense of commitment to the church and community.

The effects of modernity are aptly summarized by Ted Koontz. "Mennonites evidence a strong movement toward individualism, as reflected in rapid mobility, loosening of family ties, increase in divorce, a growing self-fulfillment emphasis, and an almost complete abandonment of the view that the church ought to have anything to say about the lives of members, either by way of discipline or mutual counsel and discernment" (Koontz, B, 415).

Our CMP data both confirm and deny this statement. Only 15% of our respondents could say that in their churches there is mutual consultation about how members live their lives. Yet 58% claimed that in their churches a sinful member is confronted. Apparently, there are standards about gross kinds of attitudes and sins but otherwise there is great leeway for private discernment about how members live their lives.

Whether because of the practice of discipline or the lack of it, our churches have high dropout rates, especially among disillusioned and critical young adults. There is a need for church renewal and restored understanding that no person can truly exercise a Christian vocation without participating in a local congregation of believers.

Nevertheless, the question of "new wineskins" for "new wine" is always before us. We dare not assume that the structures of the traditional church are essentially biblical. According to our socio-biblical criteria, there are three essential conditions for church formation. Given Christ's convening of the church and the New Testament marks of what that church should be like, we insist that to be the church a group of disciples must 1. covenant to discern a clear group purpose, 2. share the roles of leadership and partnership needed to carry out their decisions, and 3. hold each other accountable through responsible group discipline for carrying out their common mission.

Congregational discernment includes all three conditions. J. Lawrence Burkholder, retired president of Goshen College, developed the thesis that "the greatest contribution that the peace churches can make to Christendom lies in the area of the concept of the congregation." The particular dimension of congregational life which he envisioned was that of ethical discernment—the structuring of the congregation as an ethical community, making ethical decisions and implementing them in the world. "The crux of the matter," he wrote, "is the decision-making process."

The congregation of the future has to be re-formed so adult Sunday school classes and congregational meetings become more than mere forums for the exchange of ideas. Such meetings can become springboards for making binding decisions about such great issues as war, race, housing, capital punishment, unemployment, and poverty. "Congregations restructured as discerning communities would concertedly seek to meet specific needs in the world" and they "would be ordered around works of love in lowly places" (J. L. Burkholder, B, 1072-1074).

Although the structural details Burkholder describes raise many questions, one aspect of his article is undebatable. Whatever forms the churches take in our time, the crucial problem is to discern what the Lord would say to us in the congregation. "If Christ does not become a living reality within the congregation, then it would appear misleading to discuss problems that presume that he has. Better admit quite frankly that the peace churches are not certain about what constitutes obedience today and that Christian ethics in the deepest sense does not exist among them" (J. L. Burkholder, B, 1075).

Discussion Questions

1. In what sense is individualism biblical? If individualism is not all bad, what makes it bad?

2. Were you surprised to read that "Anabaptism is the essence of individualism?" What was meant by that?

3. Were you surprised that Mennonites and Brethren in Christ have been civic individualists from the beginning of their histories? Explain.

4. Which of the three indictments against the church—its being an establishment of society, its success orientation, its captivity to the sphere of residence—do you feel is the most serious weakness of churches in your denomination? Of your congregation?

5. Which of the three remedies discussed—rugged individualism, renewal, reformation—do you feel is the best response of the church to its critics?

6. Which of the three essential conditions of church formation (clear purpose, shared ministries, membership accountability) do you feel is the weakest link in your congregation?

PART C

Discernment of the Church's Ministry

How Can Pastor and People Be Partners in the Gospel?

But you are a chosen race, a royal priesthood,
a holy nation, God's own people.
—1 Peter 2:9

THE SUBTITLE OF OUR BOOK derives from the oldest image of the church in the Bible, *laos tou theou,* which is New Testament Greek for "the people of God" (Hebrews 11:25). We can begin chapter 9 by noting that our common word, *laity,* derives from the Greek *laos,* meaning "people." The image implies that the whole membership of the church—leaders and followers, pastors and laity—together constitute the *laos tou theou,* the people of God. Or as our chapter heading suggests, we are together called into partnership, into a pastor-people "sharing in the gospel" (Phil. 1:5).

But we have a problem fulfilling this partnership, a problem as old as the Old Testament. In sixteenth-century Reformation times, this problem was called clericalism. Martin Luther and the Anabaptists were known for their anticlericalism. This refers to "clerics," a somewhat negative term for clergy. The connotation is negative, not because the church does not need leaders, even ordained leaders, but because this leadership becomes a hierarchy in the church with lay people made second-class members.

Clericalism refers to the rise of an elite group in the church which usurps the ministry meant for all members. They get special favors in society, such as income tax deductions, and accumulate too much authority in the church. "They cultivate the impression that they are especially holy and that their holiness serves to make others holy" (Marty, 81-82).

The Problem of Clericalism and How It Happens

Clericalism is a good thing turned sour. There has always been a division of labor in the church. "What was everybody's job was nobody's job" (Marty, sec.1, 77). Every movement in history requires leaders, and the people of God are no exception.

The Priesthood in the Old Testament. In ancient Israel the priest was set apart as "the man who gives oracles, who tells people what the will of God is . . . who stands between the people and God and performs those rituals by which the people are assured of Yahweh's graciousness and forgiveness" (Klaassen, A, 5). At first these priestly functions were performed by any Israelite, and the covenant people of God were to be a kingdom of priests (Exod. 19:6). After the Exodus, a special group of men including Aaron and his sons were appointed by Moses to be priests to the people, assisted by the rest of the male members of the tribe of Levi. Following the conquest of Canaan, ordinary Israelites were gradually excluded from priestly functions altogether.

Then during the reigns of David and Solomon, the priests of Jerusalem, known as Zadokites, gained favored status in Israel (1 Kings 1:32-40). They become the only ones in Jerusalem who "may come near to the Lord to minister to him" (Ezek. 40:45-46). By the time of Christ, the priesthood was controlled by the descendants of Zadok, then known as the Sadducees, the supposed descendants of Aaron. They were also called the "chief priests," including one "high priest" (Mark 8:31; 14:47, etc.). They controlled the Sanhedrin, the Palestinian high court, where Jesus was tried and condemned.

The local priests throughout Palestine presided at worship and at the altar, offered the sacrifices and performed the rituals, consulted the oracle and rendered judgments, made diagnoses about suspected leprosy, and blew the trumpets in time of war. For these and other services, they were supported by tithes, offerings, and fees of various kinds.

In many ways the priests performed valid services for a congregation, faithfully teaching the people to observe all the commandments and rituals in the Law of Moses. But in their appropriation of the priesthood of all Israelites, they were vulnerable to the peril of tithing "mint, dill, and cummin," and neglecting "the weightier [spiritual and ethical] matters of the law," as Jesus said of the priests and Levites (Matt. 23:23, Luke 11:42).

Anticlericalism in the New Testament. When we move from the Old Testament to the New, we find rejection of the priesthood as a model for Christian ministry. The ministry of Jesus was continuous with that of the Hebrew prophets, especially Isaiah, who spoke of a suffering servant who would bring release to the captives and liberty to the oppressed (Luke 4:18-19; Isa. 61:1-2). The ministry of Jesus was also cast in the image of King David, in whose royal lineage he was born to be the Messiah, the "King of the Jews" (Mark 15:2, 9, 12, 18, 26) and the "King of Israel" (Mark 15:32).

But it cannot be said that in Jesus the Hebrew priest lives again. On the contrary, the chief priests were his persecutors, and his parable of the Good Samaritan painted a picture of the callous priest and Levite who turned away from a wounded man because they avoided all possibility of contact with a dead body lest it unfit them for their duties at the altar.

To be sure, the writer of Hebrews describes Jesus as both priest and high priest, but in images that indicate the very antithesis to the priests of Israel (Heb. 5:5; 7:27). There is no suggestion in Hebrews that since there was a priestly aspect to Christ's ministry, there should be a priestly role in the Christian church. Paul used the figure of the prophet to designate an important role in the church but never the figure of the priest.

New Testament anticlericalism is even more evident in the first epistle of Peter. Calling to mind the ancient concept of a kingdom of priests, Peter described the whole people of God as "a royal priesthood" (1 Pet. 2:9). This was a rejection of the hierarchical set-apart priesthood.

Clericalism in the Medieval Church. The radical anticlericalism of the New Testament gradually diminished again. By the end of the first century the set-apart priesthood reigned anew. Clement, presiding bishop of Rome, is credited with coining the term laity in A.D. 95 to refer to those who belong to the nonministerial membership. His purpose was to suppress heresy in the Corinthian church by establishing a hierarchy of leadership authority—bishop at the top, then priests, deacons, and finally laity at the bottom.

In time the bishop of Rome became the supreme pontiff and the Roman Catholic Church became the indispensable mediator of saving grace from God to the pope to the bishops to the priesthood and finally to the people. Already in Clement's letter to the Corinthian church, we have reference to an apostolic succession, the alleged unbroken transmission of leadership authority from the apostles to properly ordained priests. This succession was claimed to be essential for the valid administration of the sacraments. This development was reinforced by Ignatius, bishop of Antioch, who early in the second century wrote seven letters to the churches warning against heresy and demanding respect for the authority of their bishops.

> Let no one do anything that has to do with the church apart from the bishop. Let that be regarded as a valid eucharist which is held under the bishop or to whomever he entrusts it. Wherever the bishop appears, there let the congregation be; just as wherever Jesus Christ is, there is the whole church. It is not permissible apart from the bishop either to baptize or to celebrate the love-feast. (Schoedel, 238)

As it developed over the centuries, the division between priests and laity widened. The priest stood at communion, the laity knelt. The priest partook of both elements, the laity only of the bread. The priest was considered to be essential to the existence of the church, the laity dispensable. The sacrament could be celebrated by the priest with or without the presence of the laity.

There were several factors behind this development. In the face of heretical movements, the church seemed to need a centralized authority to protect pure doctrine. The ignorant masses of people seemed to require a system of salvation that could be mediated to them from the finished work of Christ through a proper priesthood. But behind such factors as these was "the universal anthropological drive toward the professional religionist" (Yoder, D, 44-45).

The Priesthood of Believers in Luther's Reformation. Prior to Luther, reformers John Wycliff and John Hus insisted that clergy and laity were equally essential to the nature of the church and that the cup as well as the bread should be given to the laity in the communion service. It remained for Luther to declare the Reformation principle of the priesthood of all believers.

> We are all consecrated as priests by baptism, as St. Peter says, "Ye are a royal priesthood, a holy nation" (1 Pet.ii.9); and in the Book of Revelation: "and hast made us unto our God (by Thy blood) kings and priests" (Rev. 10). . . .
> And to put the matter more plainly, if a little company of pious Christian laymen were taken prisoners and carried away to a desert, and had not among them a priest consecrated by a bishop, and were there to agree to elect one of them . . . and were to order him to baptize, to celebrate the mass, to absolve and to preach, this man would as truly be a priest, as if all the bishops and all the popes had consecrated him. (Bettenson, 274-5)

If this principle had been implemented, the pastors and people together might have truly become the discerning people of God, but it did not happen in the mainline Protestant churches. As Hendrik Kraemer wrote, "To the present day it rather fulfills the role of a flag than of an energizing, vital principle" (Kraemer, 63).

The Priesthood of All Believers in the Radical Reformation. It was among the Anabaptists that this principle was taken most seriously. For them it meant not only that priests were unnecessary as mediators between God and people but also that all members have a priestly ministry to perform in channeling the grace of God to others.

Today it is better known than before that the Anabaptists were a diverse movement best described as the Radical Reformation. According to Walter Klaassen, one attitude that identified all groups was their anticlericalism.

Anabaptism was in its time . . . part of a much larger, quite amorphous movement of popular anticlericalism. Its aim was to throw off the shackles of clerical control because they had lost confidence in the clergy as dependable spiritual guides, first the Catholic clergy, and very soon those of the "new evangelicals" (by which they meant those who were later called Protestants) as well. Mostly lay people, Anabaptists were prepared to take into their hands what had for over a millennium been reserved strictly for the clergy. (Klaassen, D, 21)

What Anabaptists took into their hands was not the Christian ministry without special leadership but rather a partnership in the gospel between pastors and people. This vision of a pastor-people partnership is illustrated in two early Anabaptist documents that circulated together in 1527— the Schleitheim "articles of brotherly union" and the articles on congregational order. One of the seven articles of brotherly union clarified the role of the pastor. Following, in parallel columns, is a comparison of that article with four of the articles on congregational order.

Brotherly Union

1. The shepherd in the church shall be a person according to the rule of Paul, fully and completely, who has a good report of those who are outside the faith. The office of such a person shall be to read and exhort and teach, warn, admonish or ban in the congregation, and properly to preside among the sisters and brothers in prayer, and in the breaking of bread, and in all things to take care of the body of Christ, that it may be built up and developed, so that the name of God might be praised and honored through us, and the mouth of the mocker be stopped.

He shall be supported, wherein he has need, by the congregation which has chosen him, so that he who serves the gospel can also live therefrom as the Lord has ordered. But should a shepherd do something worthy of reprimand, nothing shall be done with him without

Congregational Order

1. The brothers and sisters should meet at least three or four times a week, to exercise themselves in the teaching of Christ and his apostles and heartily to exhort one another to remain faithful to the Lord as they have pledged.

2. When the brothers and sisters are together, they shall take up something to read together. The one to whom God has given the best understanding shall explain it, the others should be still and listen so that there are not two or three carrying on a private conversation, bothering the others.

4. When a brother sees his brother erring, he shall warn him according to the command of Christ, and shall admonish him in a Christian and brotherly way as everyone is bound and obliged to do out of love.

7. The Lord's Supper shall be held as often as the brothers are to-

the voice of two or three witnesses. If they sin they shall be publicly reprimanded, so that others might fear. (Yoder, G, 39)

gether, thereby proclaiming the death of the Lord, and thereby warning each one to commemorate, how Christ gave his life for us, that we might also be willing to give our body and life for Christ's sake, which means for the sake of the brothers. (Yoder, G, 44-5)

In the envisioned partnership between pastor and people, all participate in "reading" (*reading* was one of the earliest words used for lay Anabaptist Bible study groups in which members shared in the reading and exposition of Scripture, normally under the leadership of one or several more knowledgeable members). All participate in the ministries of admonition and warning, although the pastor has the special authority to initiate disciplinary procedures when needed. All participate in the celebration of the Lord's Supper, although the pastor presides.

In short, pastors serve as ministers to God's ministers and as role models both within the congregation in actions binding on everyone and "outside the faith," where their moral integrity should be transparent to unbelievers as well. Here is no set-apart leadership by which one person in every congregation fulfills the ministry of the membership by proxy. If the pastor sins, two or more should bring admonition according to the rule of Christ. But if two or more members bring false witness against the pastor, they are the sinners and deserve to be disciplined themselves.

Signs of Returning Clericalism Among Mennonites. For four centuries, vestiges of the pastor-people partnership remained in the form of the plural unsalaried lay ministry in Mennonite congregations in Switzerland, South Germany, France, Holland, Poland, Prussia, Russia, North and South America. Congregations usually had multiple preachers, one or several of whom served as elder or co-elder, with more explicitly pastoral duties such as presiding at services of communion and baptism. Another ministerial office was that of deacons, serving the material needs of the members and together with the elders and preachers comprising the traditional threefold Mennonite ministry.

Yoder called this "the collegial leadership of the self-governing congregation" (Yoder, D, 39). All were chosen from the midst of the congregation by the congregation. In some congregations all were ordained to their ministry, although more often only the elders were ordained. Selection was sometimes by vote of members, sometimes by the use of the lot (after the example in Acts 1:26), and in either case usually following a nomination procedure.

Every male member was supposed to be available for call, and refusal of a call was considered a breach of the commitment made at baptism. Candidates seldom had special training for ministry apart from the catechetical instruction received for baptism. They were self-supporting, usually by farming, and served the congregation for life. Their personal qualifications for ministry were well known. Despite their weaknesses, also well known, they were given the authority needed to minister.

The cycle back toward clericalism was first observed in the Swiss-South German churches in the extraordinary authority assumed by certain elders, now called bishops, and in the early Dutch Mennonite professionalization of pastors. In the Swiss tradition, each congregation normally had its own bishop, and a congregation was not considered viable without one. Then in North America came the "diocesan bishop" with authority over multiple congregations (H. Bender, B, 704).

By the twentieth century, Mennonite congregations were gradually replacing the unpaid lay ministry with the salaried seminary-trained professional pastor. This transition was caused by several factors. One was the increasing dissatisfaction with uneducated preachers. Traditional preaching was generally of low quality. The preacher often read a sermon passed down from previous generations, or he might select a text at random after finishing Sunday morning farm chores. The members, for their part, were often too biblically illiterate to make the priesthood of all believers work. But when their educational level began to increase, they expected more from their preachers.

By now the change to the professional single-pastor system is nearly complete. Rarely anymore is the pastor elected from the midst of the congregation to serve for a lifetime without training or salary. The pastor is employed on contract for a term of two or three years, during which the pastor takes care of most ministerial duties of the congregation. Lamenting the change, one member in Holland remarked, "The beautiful simplicity is disappearing more and more from Menno's church" (Krahn, 702).

Church Renewal and the Shared Ministry. The single-pastor pattern was not adopted without some awareness of its perils for the Anabaptist vision of the shared ministry. One place the model was called into question was at the Believers Church Study Conference held on the campus of the Mennonite Biblical Seminary in Chicago in 1955. The goal of the conference was the recommitment of congregations to the Anabaptist vision of the church as a shared ministry (Pannabecker, 180-1). The resolutions that were adopted contained this paragraph:

> We feel uneasiness about the differentiation between laity and clergy in our brotherhood. Do not church members rely too heavily on the pastor? The

pastor is too often considered as the only one qualified for the task of spiritual nurture, the one paid to do the work, the members being content that
this is his job. With a salaried single-pastor ministry, have we not been di-
verted from seeking ministerial leadership from within the local congregation? May we not be losing the expectation that the Lord will raise up the
leadership gifts required in our own congregation? (BC, 11)

Conference delegates realized that restoring the unpaid, untrained
lay ministry was not the solution. Several reported bad experiences with
authoritarian elders in their home congregations, claiming that the shift
to the professional pastor pattern had actually resulted in a more fraternal relationship between minister and congregation.

Even though a minister is called from the outside, we need ever to avoid the
feeling of class distinction, and we should consider the minister as simply
one of the members. There must be that close, fraternal feeling of belonging
together. . . . Love and goodwill is the bond which unites the minister and
the people, enabling them to be co-workers together with God in the great
task of the kingdom. (BC, 11)

In the late 1950s, the Chicago Seminary merged with the Goshen
College Biblical Seminary to become the Associated Mennonite Biblical
Seminaries in Elkhart, Indiana. One of the first items on the faculty agenda was to develop a curriculum true to the Anabaptist vision of shared
ministry. In an intensive two-year curricular revision, the faculty made a
radical recommitment to a multiple ministry in which

every member has a ministry (Rom. 12:4-8; 1 Cor. 12:4-31; Eph. 4:4-16), [a
ministry that] is not just his [or her] gainful employment in the secular
realm but a task to be done in the corporate life of the congregation, in its
worship, in its teaching, its preaching, its discernment of God's will, in its
government, and in its service in the world. These tasks are specifically assigned, multiple in the sense that the church's mission requires a variety of
persons to work in unity rather than a variety of functions to be assigned to
one "minister." (R. Bender, 154)

The overarching purpose of the new curriculum was to prepare men
and women for the ministry of all believers. In principle the presence of
an ordained pastor was not assumed essential to the "being" of the
church but was part of its "well-being." Indeed, the faculty questioned
whether the dominance of the set-apart pastor was undermining the
shared ministry vision in some congregations.

The concentration of training, prestige, and remuneration in one person has
not contributed as effectively to the realization of our view of ministry and
the equipping of all Christians for mission as would be desirable. The emer-
gence of formal theological training programs with their borrowed patterns

has further contributed to the undue concentration of leadership responsibility in one person. (R. Bender, 155)

The seminaries continued to train persons for salaried pastorates with a new emphasis on becoming "servants of God's servants" (P. Miller).

Then in the early 1980s the seminaries entered a new stage of curricular adjustment in which training for several basic professional ministries became the predominant focus. In principle this was not a return to the single-pastor pattern, nor antagonistic toward the radical view of the multiple ministry. It stemmed from the same shared ministry principles of Romans 12, 1 Corinthians 12, and Ephesians 4, previously affirmed.

However, in the previous curriculum, the faculty were perhaps overly impressed with the discoveries that to each is given a gift (1 Cor. 12:7) and that each member's gift is essential (v. 22). They thus unwittingly neglected the realism in those same passages that some members are indeed "weaker" (vv. 22-24) and that others are especially needed for the well-being of the congregation "to equip God's people for work in his ministry, to the building up of the body of Christ" (Eph. 4:12, NEB). This applied especially to such gifts as pastor in verse 11 and to whatever else Paul meant by "leader" in Romans 12:8.

The quest for a workable model for the biblical pastor-people partnership continues, and it cannot be said that the seminaries and churches have yet put it all together (Peachey, 1-2). As was said of Luther's principle of the priesthood of all believers, the seminaries' vision of the shared ministry still serves more the role of a flag than of an energizing vital principle.

Meanwhile, in the denominations jointly sponsoring the Church Member Profile research project, there have been various calls for a return to a more Anabaptist pattern. In an article published in all of the Mennonite and BIC papers, Katie Funk Wiebe asked in all seriousness, "Can the church survive the professionalization of its leadership?" She notes how our churches have been changing from spiritual entity to business enterprise, from organism to organization, from servant leadership to professionals paid to do a job, from body of Christ to institution.

> Now the number of professionals on church staffs is growing, and the laity is meekly subsiding into the pews. The church as a bustling institution with efficient, effective hired professionals at its helm is too often more apparent than is Christ's glorious body of faithful believers where every member is a minister. (K. Wiebe, 124)

Wiebe compares the hankering for professional pastors to the longing of the ancient Israelites for a king (1 Sam. 10:17-19). She quotes Mennonite Brethren Seminary professor Al Dueck, who observes that "the experts have taken control, adjudicated needs, nurtured dependence, and sapped resources. Meanwhile, lay persons have lost their ability to think and act for themselves" (Dueck, 202). Wiebe believes that lay members have convinced themselves that they cannot participate in the preaching ministry, have disenfranchised themselves, and are consequently confused about their verbal witness responsibilities.

The whole range of attitudes about the pastor-people relationship was represented in our interviews with CMP II respondents.

> *Sally Mae Stauffer, separatist.* We wouldn't know what to do in our church if we didn't have our minister and elders. The elders take over when the minister is sick; but if they were all sick at the same time, I guess we would call the minister at Atwater for help.
>
> *Glenn Klassen, conservative.* I certainly have never seen the "P.C." sign in the sky saying "preach Christ." If I had, for me it would have meant "plant corn." I think of my ministry, if it can be said that I have one, as working my farm as a call of God and as living and being a witness in our community. I expect our minister to help me to see the bearing of the Christian faith in my occupation and community life, but for him to do so I need to give him feedback on how his sermons do or do not speak to my situation.
>
> *Denise Preheim, liberal.* When I spoke to our pastor about my sense of call to the pastoral ministry, he encouraged me to go to seminary but warned me that the churches were probably not ready for female pastors. He said there were other church-sponsored ministries that would offer open doors for me, such as the DCE [director of Christian education], youth ministry, or overseas missionary service.
>
> I said, "If what you've been saying is true, that there are seven pastoral vacancies in our district right now and that the shortage of pastoral candidates is going to get worse before it gets better, how can the church continue to waste the leadership potential of us women who are willing to serve? I have many ideas of what I could do in the pastoral ministry by working together with other members."
>
> *Menno Isaac, transformist.* We're certainly not closed to the possibility of hiring a pastor in our Fellowship, and I'm sure we could afford one, at least on a half-time basis. I see us gradually moving in that direction, but right now the voluntary shared ministry is functioning okay and keeps us from sitting back and letting the professional do it all. I think it would be a good experience for every church to have interim periods without a regular pastor so they could recapture the biblical vision of ministry and rediscover that a church's existence doesn't depend on having an ordained minister.

Gauging Commitment to a Shared Ministry in the Church

In the Church Member Profile questionnaire, several statements were included to gauge attitudes about clericalism and commitment to a shared ministry in the church.

A church congregation cannot be complete unless there is an ordained minister to lead the congregation and perform the ministerial functions.

A proper view of congregational leadership is that all members should share, as they are able, in the ministerial functions of the congregation.

Overall two-thirds of the members agreed that all members should share in ministerial functions. Conversely, slightly less than half agreed that ordained ministers should lead and perform the ministerial functions for *the church to be complete*. This indicates a considerable ambiguity among respondents on the issues of this chapter. Some respondents probably affirmed both statements. Indeed, our quest has been the integration of the reciprocal roles of pastor and people.

We discovered, moreover, that the traditional separatist members are most committed to a single-pastor pattern of ministry. Conversely, the transformist members are most committed to the shared ministry pattern. This is understandable, for many members of transformist churches are part of an urban fellowship lacking financial resources to support a full-time professional pastor without support from the denomination, and some prefer to be self-supporting. Thus they have to be willing to share in the church's ministry and leadership.

Conclusion: Toward a Model of the Pastor-People Partnership

Three marvelous images of the pastor-people partnership from Paul's letter to the Ephesians are "the unity of the Spirit" (4:3), "the fullness of Christ" (4:13) and "the whole body . . . working properly" (4:3, 13, 16, RSV). What would such a pastor-people partnership look like in operation? The basic principle needing to be implemented is the mutual participation of pastor and people in *all* the traditional functions of the Christian ministry.

This can be illustrated by reference to one of the traditional ministries—preaching. A skill a professional pastor can be expected to have is to prepare and preach a sermon. But the most expert exposition of a biblical text and the most polished delivery of a sermon can fail to be the kind of "preaching in the Spirit" that enables a congregation to discern how that particular "Word of God" transforms their particular human situation.

Application to the human situation can best be made in dialogue with the sermon, either as part of the worship service or in a subsequent dialogue session. If the sermon is worth all the hours of preparation, it is worth discussing afterward. And so another principle of the pastor-people partnership is that most, if not all, of the sermons preached from the pulpit should have meaningful response from the congregation. Those responses could be at the feeling or the intellectual level.

The other crucial part of "the whole body . . . working properly" is the discernment of preaching gifts of others in the congregation. A feasible goal would be to commission up to ten percent of the members for occasional preaching of sermons from the pulpit. Now the role of the pastor is to resource and equip these persons to prepare and preach their sermons, scheduling one every month or two (Neufeld, A, 677).

This two-directional partnership can be summarized in the following pair of interrelationships.

> 1. The pastor as servant of the Word and the laity as respondents and enablers.
> 2. The laity as servants of the Word and the pastor as enabler and equipper.

This kind of pattern could work with the other congregational ministries as well. In short, a pastor's master role is that of servant of the body life of the fellowship. Pastors offer the resources of their libraries, the knowledge of their seminary educations, and the skills gained through experience to supply what the laity need for discipleship and ministries—biblical and theological understanding and churchly know-how.

Discussion Questions

1. Why do you think there appears to be "a universal anthropological drive toward the professional religionist"? What's wrong with that?

2. Why did the Old Testament priesthood turn sour in Jesus' time? Didn't the prophetic and kingly ministries have equally negative forms?

3. What were some factors explaining the rise of the authority of the bishop in the medieval church? Are these factors still at work today?

4. Why was Luther's "priesthood of all believers" so largely stillborn in Reformation times? How could the Anabaptists make it work when the other Protestant churches failed?

5. Why did some Mennonite bishops become so authoritarian, creating a gulf between themselves and their people?

6. Do you believe our seminaries are training pastors to be partners with the congregations that call them?

7. It is sometimes said that rank-and-file members of congregations do not have the time or talents to be co-workers with their pastors. Do you agree?

8. Do you personally have at least one spiritual gift for ministry? If so, what is it? Do you feel you can exercise this gift in partnership with the ministries of your pastor? Do you agree or disagree with the author's comment that perhaps ten percent of lay members of our churches have the gifts to preach sermons with the help of their pastors? Should they be given opportunity to exercise that gift?

CHAPTER 10

Should Women Have Equal Opportunity for Church Leadership?

There is no longer . . . male and female;
for all of you are one in Christ Jesus.
—Galatians 3:28

IN THIS CHAPTER, the objective is to help congregations discern how the biblical community of faith (as defined in chapter 4) addresses an issue like the leadership of women in the church. This is currently one of the most pressing issues in the participant CMP denominations.

In the Mennonite Brethren Church, moderator Herbert Brandt, speaking for his Board of Reference and Counsel, cited women in ministry as a major unfinished agenda item for the 1990-93 triennium (Brandt, 16). In the Mennonite Church, the Commission on Congregational Leadership under the Board of Congregational Ministries prioritized its agenda for the biennium, and the issue of women in congregational leadership was put at the top of the list.

Church Member Profile Findings

In the CMP II survey, church members responded to four questions on this subject.

1. Which of the following responsibilities or duties do you think are appropriate for women to fill in congregational leadership? Place a check mark in front of each item that you feel is appropriate for a qualified woman:
____deacon or deaconess
____worship leader
____youth minister
____ordained minister

_____chairperson of a church council
_____chairperson of a board of elders
_____minister of Christian education
_____preaching
_____reading and interpreting Scripture (worship service)
_____conduct weddings
_____conduct communion service
_____conduct baptisms
_____conduct funerals
_____conduct ordinations

2. In the future should larger numbers of qualified women be elected or appointed to church boards and committees at denominational, district, and congregational levels? 1. No. 2. Undecided. 3. Yes.

3. Should the policy on ordinations in your denomination allow for the ordination of women to the Christian ministry? 1. No. 2. Uncertain. 3. Yes.

4. Do you believe that women in Canadian and American societies are being discriminated against and denied certain basic rights? 1. No. 2. Uncertain. 3. Yes.

On the first question, which we called the women-in-church leadership scale, members scored anywhere from 0 to 14, depending on how many of the fourteen responsibilities were checked as appropriate for qualified women. Questions 2-4 were combined into a secondary role-of-women scale. The number assigned to the respondent's answer to each question was his or her numerical score for that item—one for a "no" response, two for "uncertain" or "undecided," and three for a "yes" response. Then by totaling a respondent's scores to all three items, the computer could give each member a total role-of-women scale score on a range from 3 to 9.

We found large differences between the four types of churches, especially in the women-in-church leadership scale. In fact the differences are greater on this issue than on most other questions probed. On the average, members of the separatist churches check less than five of the fourteen leadership roles as appropriate for women while the members of the liberal churches approve more than thirteen, the overall average being nine.

The conference leaders quoted at the beginning of this chapter are right—this is a controversial issue needing resolution. Large numbers of members responded to the role of women questions by checking "uncertain" or "undecided." It appear that this undecided group especially needs help to sort out the issues. In the rest of this chapter, we will try to facilitate the discernment process by examining the biblical options as viewed from the perspective of conservative-reactionary and progressive-radical types of church members.

The Biblical Views of Women

"With this issue," writes Willard Swartley, "we come to a contemporary storm center in biblical interpretation." Swartley asks four questions.

> Does the Bible teach a specific hierarchy and prescribed roles for men and women?
> Or is the Bible itself a liberating resource for role-oppressed women and men?
> Does Scripture command women to be veiled and silent in public worship, thus excluding them from leadership ministry, especially ordination?
> Or does Scripture welcome and even commend women in an unrestricted variety of Christian ministries dependent upon gifts and calling? (Swartley, 150)

Perhaps one reason the members of the five participant CMP denominations are so divided in their attitudes on the issue is that the Bible itself seems to give mixed signals. Indeed, as Swartley shows, it is easy for representatives of the conservative-reactionary and progressive-radical points of view to find proof texts to support their opposing arguments.

> 1. *Progressive-Radical Text: Genesis 1:26-27*
> Then God said, "Let us make humankind in our image, according to our likeness; and let them have dominion over the fish of the sea, and over the birds of the air, and over the cattle, and over all the wild animals of the earth, and over every creeping thing that creeps upon the earth."
> So God created humankind in his image, in the image of God he created them; male and female he created them.

In the New Revised Standard Version of this text, the word "humankind" replaces the older translation, "man," because it includes both men and women without discrimination. This is further substantiated by the use of the plural "them" before "male and female" are mentioned. Humankind—male and female—is created in the image of God, not by command alone as in the case of the other creatures but by act of counsel, "Let us make humankind in our image, according to our likeness."

The words "image" and "likeness" combine to express resemblance to the Creator God. This resemblance is not the bodily form of man and woman but has rather to do with their capacity for a covenant relationship with God based on a rational awareness of the reality of a personal Creator God.

Because of the divine image in humankind, the first mandate given to woman and man is to have dominion over the lesser creatures. Theologians call this the "cultural mandate" by which "every human being is equally responsible under God for all aspects of life on this earth" including such endeavors as "agriculture, animal husbandry, education, industry, government, commerce, the arts" (Swartley, 152-153, citing Scan-zoni/ Hardesty, 24-25). Having dominion over God's creation is entrust-ed to humankind in the plural, not in the singular. On the basis of this text, progressives and radicals refer to the male-female relationship as a partnership of equals (Swartley, 184).

> 2. *Conservative-Reactionary Text: Genesis 2:18, 21-24*
> Then the Lord God said, "It is not good that the man should be alone; I will make him a helper as his partner" . . . So the Lord God caused a deep sleep to fall upon the man, and he slept; then he took one of his ribs and closed up its place with flesh. And the rib that the Lord God had taken from the man he made into a woman and brought her to the man. Then the man said, "This at last is bone of my bones and flesh of my flesh; and this one shall be called Woman, for out of Man this one was taken. Therefore a man leaves his father and his mother and clings to his wife, and they become one flesh.

The implications of this text are that the woman was created for the man. Man therefore has authority over the one who is to be his helper. On the basis of this text, Stephen Clark gives three reasons why women should be subordinate. Man is at the center of the story; humanity (man) is identified with the male and not with the female; and man was created first, giving him a natural precedence (Swartley, 154, citing Clark, 24-25).

Conservative/reactionary interpreters refer to the two Genesis texts as a unit, assuming that what was written in Genesis 2 is consistent with Genesis 1.

> 3. *Conservative-Reactionary Texts: 1 Corinthians 11:3-10; 14:33b-36*
> But I want you to understand that Christ is the head of every man, and the husband is the head of his wife, and God is the head of Christ. Any man who prays or prophesies with something on his head disgraces his head, but any woman who prays or prophesies with her head unveiled disgraces her head—it is one and the same thing as having her head shaved. . . . For a man ought not to have his head veiled, since he is the image and reflection of God; but woman is the reflection of man. Indeed, man was not made from woman, but woman from man. Neither was man created for the sake of woman, but woman for the sake of man. . . .
> (As in all the churches of the saints, women should be silent in the churches. For they are not permitted to speak, but should be subordinate, as the law also says. If there is anything they desire to know, let them ask their husbands at home. For it is shameful for a woman to speak in church.)

It is obvious Paul based these admonitions on the Genesis 2 text, par-ticularly the pair of suppositions that woman was made from man who therefore has precedence, and that woman was made for man and is therefore subordinate. Thus Paul condemns the efforts of the Corinthian women to have equal status with their husbands as contrary to God's cre-ation.

Conservative-reactionary interpreters ground Paul's teachings in a so-called order of creation specified in the Genesis 2 account rather than in a particular cultural context in Corinth. Therefore, because of a perceived natural difference between men and women, they interpret his admonitions as normative for all times and places.

Paul's counsel for women to be silent in church is likewise grounded in the so-called Genesis law concerning the subordination of women. Here he is moving the discussion from the order of creation to appropriate or inappropriate roles in worship and in congregational meetings. As a kind of last word on the subject, woman's subjection to man is compared with Christ's subjection to God.

4. *Progressive-Radical Text: Galatians 3:28*
There is no longer Jew or Greek, there is no longer slave or free, there is no longer male and female; for all of you are one in Christ Jesus.

Progressive-radical interpreters consider this verse a high point in New Testament theology even as Genesis 1:26-27 was regarded as a high point of revelation in the Old Testament. They see Paul's Galatian text in the context of a progressive discernment process from a restricted to an unrestricted view of women's roles in the church. Evidence for the theory of a progression in Paul's view of women is found in the fact that in the restrictive Corinthian texts he appealed to the second Creation narrative (Gen. 2:18-14), while here he presupposes the Genesis 1 account. Thus the progressive interpreters observe an inner tension in Paul between his traditional rabbinic perspective and the fullness of Christ's gospel (see Eph. 4:13).

Progressive-radical interpreters consider the attitude of Jesus toward women to have been revolutionary. On the other side of the argument, conservative-reactionary interpreters cite the fact that Jesus chose twelve men to be his most intimate disciples as a reason to restrict the ordained ministry to men. Nevertheless, Jesus entrusted vital roles in his kingdom movement to women.

Like Jesus, Paul was remarkably free to have a "partnership in the gospel" with women like Euodia and Syntyche, who "have labored side by side with me in the gospel" (Phil. 1:5; 4:3). In Romans 16, Paul named ten women including Junia, a person of note among the apostles. In this closing chapter, he mentions such women as Phoebe, "a deaconess of the church at Cenchreae" (v. 1); Prisca, wife of Aquila, "my fellow workers in Christ Jesus" (v. 3); Mary, "who has worked hard among you" (v. 6); and Tryphaena and Tryphosa, "workers in the Lord" (v. 12). (All Scripture in this paragraph from RSV.)

So how are we to think about the mixed signals left to us by Paul in his letters to the churches? John Neufeld calls Galatians 3:28 a "break-through" (Neufeld, B, 28-32) and "recognizes a tension between the kingdom vision and the cultural reality, which in Paul's time kept him from fully implementing the radically new vision. . . ." (Swartley, 166). Paul Jewett believes that the Galatians text "shows that Paul fundamentally agrees with Jesus, even though elsewhere he backs off from implementing his vision" (Swartley, 166, citing Jewett, 142-145).

These, of course, are progressive points of view. There is a strong disposition on both sides to interpret the texts to fit one's prior presuppositions. Thus, for example, a conservative interpretation of the Galatians text might affirm that in Christ, men and women have equal access to salvation while holding to the subordination of women in the order of creation. On the other hand, a progressive view of the 1 Corinthians 11 text might argue that when Paul admonished the Corinthian women to wear the veil at all times, he was really giving them the authority thereby to lead out in prayer and to prophesy, as suggested in verse 5.

The problem with such interpretations is that they tend to force coherency when it is fairly obvious that in his references to women Paul was expressing considerable ambivalence. By taking the Pauline texts at face value, we can more pertinently interpret this ambivalence as an unresolved discernment process which, unlike that concerning the Jew-Gentile relationship, was only beginning to be played out.

The Unresolved Discernment Process in the Early Church

When we take a question like this to the Bible for guidance, we would be well advised to ask whether this issue was faced and resolved by the early church, faced but not resolved, or not even experienced in the early church in the way it confronts the church today. For example, as we saw in chapter 5, the question of Jew-Gentile relationships was confronted and resolved at the Jerusalem Conference (Acts 15). The issue of male-female relations and women's leadership was addressed in various ways but never fully resolved. Some issues like interdenominational or inter-Mennonite relationships are contemporary issues for which we can only look for principles or perhaps remote parallels in the Scriptures.

The way the early biblical community processed the issue of Jew-Gentile relationships gives us a model for the way we can work at resolving the question of a shared ministry between men and women. As in our own meetings, the participants in that Conference came to Jerusalem with presuppositions conditioned by their experiences and temperaments. There were at least two attitudes at Jerusalem, which in chapter 5 we labeled as conservative and progressive. Both positions had an element of truth that needed sorting and integrating.

There were elements of both attitudes in the mind of Paul on various issues, just as there often is in each of us, but on the issue of Jew-Gentile relationships in the church, he was decidedly a progressive. In that biblical community, he confronted Peter not for being a conservative, but for vacillating between tradition and revision and thereby giving mixed signals. As he wrote in Galatians 2:11, "I opposed him to his face, because he was clearly in the wrong" (NEB).

When we return to the issue of the leadership of women, searching Scripture for guidance, we discover fascinating clues. It was clearly an issue the early church was beginning to face as women like Lydia in Philippi, Priscilla in Corinth and Ephesus, Phoebe in Cenchreae, and others, emerged as gifted leaders. However, the issue was not brought to resolution so far as we read in the New Testament canon.

On this issue it was not Peter but Paul who was giving mixed signals. Paul worked in partnership with numerous women already mentioned. But when he faced a problem in the Corinthian church of certain arrogant women who dominated the shared worship, Paul reacted and wrote "the women should be silent in the churches." Some commentators interpret this text as a reaction to a specific problem in the Corinthian church, as suggested by the KJV: "Let your women keep silence." Be this as it may, Paul seemed intent on making a general application of his teaching "in all the churches of the saints."

His ambivalence is noticeable in two other respects when we compare the two Corinthian texts. In the first, Paul speaks of proper head coverings for women when they pray or prophesy—surely verbal ministries in public worship. In the second, women should not address the meeting at all. In the first, after saying that man was not made from woman, but woman from man, Paul goes on to proclaim, "Nevertheless, in the Lord woman is not independent of man or man independent of woman. For just as woman came from man, so man came through woman; but all things come from God" (1 Cor. 11:11-12). This insertion seems to suggest that in the order of cocreation, man comes from woman as much as woman from man, indicating their interdependence and mutuality *in the Lord*.

Summary and Conclusion

When we confront the issue of women's leadership in our congregations today, how are we to view these mixed signals from the New Testament? First, we accept the mandate given us by Christ to function as a biblical community, after the example of the early church, using *all* the gifts of the Spirit. "The eye cannot say to the hand, 'I have no need of you,' nor the head to the feet, 'I have no need of you' " (1 Cor. 12:21). We have the mandate to try to resolve what in this case the early church left unresolved (John 16:12-15).

Second, we acknowledge that the human, cultural level of interpretation by which Paul was reacting to the Corinthian problem needs to be tested by the higher "in the Lord" level of interpretation, as he himself acknowledged (1 Cor. 11:11). On the level of "nature" or "culture" (1 Cor. 11:14), Paul was a traditionalist on male-female relationships, but "in the Lord" he was moving in a progressive direction when compared with existing customs in Greco-Roman society.

The problem is not that Paul affirmed both points of view, but that he seems to have vacillated between them, just as Peter did on the issue of Jew-Gentile relationships. So far as we know from the New Testament, no person emerged in that biblical community to confront Paul about this as he had confronted Peter. Had that happened, there are reasons to assume he would have accepted correction. He readily confessed that he saw some things "as in a mirror dimly" (1 Cor. 13:12), that he had not attained perfection (Phil. 3:12), that "the love of Christ . . . surpasses knowledge" (Eph. 3:19). He acknowledged that on some issues, like divorce, he had a word from the Lord (1 Cor. 7:10) but that on other issues, like celibacy, he spoke his own opinion and "not that of the Lord" (v. 12).

In no way does Paul's awareness of his own fallibility undermine his authority as an apostle or the authority of his writings as part of New Testament Scripture. On every issue on which he wrote, the Word of God breaks through. As Swartley writes, the fact that he gave "mixed signals, especially on the surface of the [particular] text . . . is due not to the nature of God but to the fact that divine revelation comes into and through history and culture" (Swartley, 203).

Nor do we show disrespect for the authority of the Bible as the Word of God when we pick up anew our mandate to act as the biblical community on issues like this today. On the contrary, we have this mandate from the Lord of the church, who promised to send us the Holy Spirit, who will teach you everything and remind you of all that I have said to you" (John 14:26).

So how do we proceed to discuss and discern this issue? We begin by acknowledging that there are at least two opposing points of view within the church. Swartley has labeled these positions "hierarchical" and "liberationist." We have used the terms "conservative-reactionary" and "progressive-radical."

The conservative follows Paul back to the second Creation story and concludes that the husband should rule over the wife (1 Cor. 14:34; Gen. 3:16). The progressive observes, however, that in Gen. 3:16, the domination of man over woman is rooted in the fall and the curse, and not in the order of creation. The first Creation narrative declares that man and woman alike are created in the image of God for interdependence and joint responsibility for the cultural mandate—"let them have dominion" (Gen.1:26).

Given such diverse points of view, is it possible for the biblical community to reach a consensus on this issue? Our four CMP II representatives expressed such diverse attitudes that we can only admit that the discernment process will be difficult.

Sally Mae Stauffer, separatist. Most people in our church would never want women as deacons, let alone as pastors. We take the Word literally that the man is created for headship and the woman for child nurture and serving. My head covering indicates my place in this respect. I would always want to look up to a man as my pastor or my elder.

Glenn Klassen, conservative. On your list of responsibilities appropriate for women in the church, I checked four—deaconess, worship leader, minister of Christian education, and reading and interpreting Scripture, so long as it wasn't done behind the pulpit. I believe the pulpit is reserved for the pastor, and the ordination of women is just not being done in the Mennonite Brethren Church.

I've never known a woman who even wanted to be a pastor. We have a lady here who is minister of Christian education, and there is talk that she would like to be ordained. But as often as I've talked to her, I've never had the impression that she wanted to preach or anything like that. She wants to minister in her own area, the Christian teaching of children.

Denise Preheim, liberal. Let's face it: women are just as strong in their spiritual aptitude as men. If a woman has the spiritual gift to preach and to pastor, I don't see how the church can forbid it and be true to the highest teaching of the Bible. Sooner or later we're going to have a search committee looking for a new pastor, and the best candidate on their list will be a woman. The truth will prevail and the times will change. Like the old saying, "people who stand in the way of progress get run over."

Menno Isaac, transformist. We wouldn't even discuss the issue in our Fellowship, because it's not a question on which we disagree. When the time comes to hire a pastor, I suppose the only question that might come up is whether we should take the affirmative-action approach and deliberately go after a woman just because there are so few openings for women pastors in our churches.

If the Jerusalem Conference is a model for how the congregation or conference finds resolution of a problem as complex and emotional as this, the answer is, "Yes, it is possible, by the guidance of the Holy Spirit." But there has to be a chastening of people on both sides of the issue. This can come through the testimony and storytelling of persons who have witnessed God's dealings with both men and women in church leadership. Congregations who have called and ordained women as pastors have a responsibility to bear witness to what they believe to be true without any note of arrogance. If the discernment process is located in a conference of multiple congregations, there can be mutual witness and admonition growing out of the four attitudes representing the four types of church described at the beginning of this chapter.

Despite his obvious ambivalence, Paul proclaimed the ultimate principle and imperative when he wrote, "There is no longer male and female; for all of you are one in Christ Jesus" (Gal. 3:28). Despite its leaning in the direction of the hierarchical interpretation, the 1963 *Mennonite Confession of Faith* also makes claim to this higher principle and moral imperative. "We believe that in their relation to the Lord, men and women are equal, for in Christ there is neither male nor female" (MCF, 52).

Despite the tensions emerging over this issue in the district conferences of our denominations, we too will find the higher principle and moral imperative. We may not arrive at uniformity of practice among the congregations but may attain a mutual respect. We hope we can affirm the Christian biblical integrity of congregations that have different positions about women serving as pastors, so long as the unity of the body of Christ is preserved.

Discussion Questions

1. Why, in your opinion, are the four kinds of Mennonite and Brethren in Christ churches so far apart on the question of women in church leadership?

2. Does the Bible teach a specific hierarchy and prescribed roles for men and women? Or is the Bible a liberating resource for role-oppressed men and women?

3. Is it possible to reject Paul's command for women to be silent in church without undermining his authority as an apostle and the authority of the Bible?

4. Does Paul's assertion that in Christ there is no longer male and female imply that women should have equal opportunity for church leadership, including the possibility of ordination to the ministry? How should the mixed signals that came from Paul's writings on this subject be interpreted?

5. How is the Jerusalem Council (Acts 15) a model for the congregational discernment of women's roles in the church? Is it possible for opposing sides to reach a compromise on this issue like they did at the Jerusalem Conference? What might such a compromise look like?

Discernment of the Christian's Discipleship

CHAPTER 11

How Can Christians Be Peacemakers?

*Blessed are the peacemakers, for they
will be called children of God.*
—Matthew 5:9

THE MOST WIDELY KNOWN CHARACTERISTIC of the peoples called Mennonites and Brethren in Christ is their pacifism (Mead, 58-59, 136-140). The term derives from the Latin *pax* (peace) and *facere* (to make), meaning literally *peacemaking* (D. Brown, 4). The widely used phrase *historic peace church* did not come into vogue until 1935. However, the Mennonites, Quakers, and Brethren were the three main historic peace churches who from the beginning of their histories believed that peacemaking, including the resolve not to participate in warfare, is a mandate from Christ to his disciples (Matt. 5:9, 21-22, 38-47).

Varieties of Pacifism

The term *pacifism* has been used to refer to many kinds of peacemaking. As one Mennonite scholar observed, "Some modern pacifists who oppose all wars find their authority in the will of God and in the word of Scripture, while others find it largely in human reason" (Hershberger, B, 104).

There are significant differences even among the historic peace churches. Commenting on the different nuances in the pacifism of Mennonites, Brethren, and Quakers, a Brethren scholar observes several characteristics of the Mennonite peace position. It is grounded in the biblicism of the sixteenth-century evangelical Anabaptists, focused on the lordship of Jesus Christ, defined as the way of nonresistance and the cross, and expressed in a humble peaceful lifestyle. The Mennonite way of life has been described by the German word *Gelassenheit*, meaning peaceableness (or yieldedness). Mennonites have been guided by a two-kingdom ethic—the life of the heavenly kingdom in the midst of a fallen earthly kingdom (D. Brown, 41ff.). For Mennonites, who are the pessimists among the historic peace churches,

> nonresistance is not based on any pragmatic conviction that it will win the war or melt the hearts of the enemy or anything else of that sort; it is based on the eschatological (future-oriented) conviction at the very heart of the Christian faith that the future is in Jesus Christ and that therefore we can accept whatever that future might bring without regard for ourselves, even though it bring a cross. (D. Brown, 43; G. Kaufman, 24)

The Quakers (or Society of Friends) are the charismatics of the peace tradition, grounding their peace testimony in the Holy Spirit of Christ's abiding presence in the world. They believe this presence is the "seed of Christ in all people." Thus they are more optimistic than Mennonites that the power of the Holy Spirit can transform our fallen world and usher in manifestations of justice, peace, and righteousness. This happens through what Quakers call "the Lamb's war" (see Rev. 17:14), defined as "an eternal, prophetic, missionary, evangelistic, ideological, social, economic, and political struggle against evil in human history until God in mercy brings history to the peaceable kingdom promised by Isaiah and described in Revelation" (Brown, 45).

The Brethren peace position seeks to blend the somber *Gelassenheit* of the Mennonites with the more spirited Quaker peacemaking emphasis. The Brethren stance is more institutionally ecumenical than either and tries to bring a peace witness to the nonpacifist denominations in the national and world councils of churches. The Brethren believe that "it is possible for the peace witness to embody both the nonresistance [of the Mennonites] and the nonviolent resistance [of the Quakers]. To the picture of Jesus as one who 'when he was reviled . . . did not revile in return' . . . might be added the story of how he overturned the tables in the temple" (D. Brown, 48).

Variations Within Mennonite and Brethren in Christ Churches

These observations notwithstanding, there are as many differences within Mennonite and BIC congregations as there are between them and the other peace churches. For the sake of testing and gauging, using CMP questionnaire responses we can identify two broad types, which we will label "traditional isolationist Mennonite pacifism" and "emergent aggressive Mennonite peacemaking."

Traditional Isolationist Mennonite Pacifism. When their century-old privileges of exemption from military service were revoked in the early

1870s, Russian Mennonites looked to the United States and Canada as the next possible destination in their perennial pilgrimage "through this barren land" (to use a line from an old hymn). They were wooed by agents of the American railroads, who had vast land grants from the government to sell in alternate mile-square sections in the prairie states of Kansas, Nebraska, and Minnesota.

Desiring to transplant their communal colonization system, the Russian Mennonites desired access also to the sections in between. This required a special act of Congress to set aside up to 500,000 acres so that the Russian Mennonites could settle in separate enclaves, just like they had in Russia.

In the early weeks of 1874, the senators debated Bill 655 "to enable the Mennonites from Russia to effect permanent settlement on the public lands of the United States." Naturally, the senators from the prairie states waxed eloquent in their arguments for the bill—the opportunity to obtain a high class of immigrants who were among the world's best wheat growers and a peace-loving people who make good citizens wherever they live, and the desire to offer asylum to an often-persecuted religious minority group.

Arguments against the bill were equally persuasive—opposition to the traditional separatism of the Mennonites, their semiautonomous subculture, their tendency to monopolize large blocks of farmland, and especially their refusal to bear arms in the common defense of the nation. Oris Sanford Ferry, a brigadier general in the Civil War, rose to his feet and shouted his objection to the bill.

> Mr. President, the real point in this bill has not been touched. The Mennonites' difficulty with the Russian Government consists simply in this: They, in their religious tenets, are opposed to war and refuse to enter the military service of a great military power. They desire to emigrate somewhere where they will be free from the obligation of defending by physical force the nationality of which they are members; and this bill is so drawn that the Mennonites who come to this country under it may take up these lands and hold them indefinitely without ever becoming liable to compulsory military service if the Government of the United States should be compelled to call upon them in time of war. (Correll, 192)

Thomas W. Tipton, the senior senator from Nebraska, whose state stood to gain much from the Mennonite immigration, took the floor and turned the somberness of the chamber to raucous laughter by asking,

> In God's name, have we not enough of the fighting element in America? Just look to Arkansas, where the people are never happy unless they are in a fight! Our people are a peculiar people; and if there is any portion of the world that can send us a few advocates of peace, in God's name let us bid

them welcome. We want settlers of that kind. (Correll, 219-20)

This kind of faint praise is reminiscent of the words of a prominent Christian ethicist, who characterized the Mennonite peace position as "a strategy of withdrawal" (Bennett, 41ff.). He believed that pure pacifist types like the Mennonites are needed as witnesses to the way of the cross of Christ, even though that position is otherwise naive and irrelevant to the issues of social injustice throughout the world.

The traditional Mennonite peace position has been clearly defined in the writings of Mennonite scholar Guy F. Hershberger, for whom the term nonresistance best expresses the Mennonite position. "The term nonresistance . . . describes the faith and life of those who accept the Scriptures as the revealed will of God and who cannot have any part in warfare because they believe the Bible forbids it, and who renounce all coercion, even *nonviolent coercion*" (Hershberger, A, 203; italics added).

For Hershberger, the New Testament doctrine of nonresistance is best understood in distinction to modern pacifism.

> Modern pacifism sees peace as an end in itself, whereas the doctrine of nonresistance sees it as the fruit of regenerated Christians living in obedience to Jesus Christ.
>
> Modern pacifism tends to be optimistic concerning its possible achievements, while the doctrine of nonresistance reckons with the reality of sin and does not assume the peaceful transformation of an unregenerate social order.
>
> Modern pacifism seeks the benevolent administration of the state by Christian principles, while the doctrine of nonresistance sees the basic purpose of the state as the maintenance of social order by coercive means in a fallen sinful society.
>
> Modern pacifism tends to compromise with the coercive methods of the state, while the doctrine of nonresistance holds fast to the high love ethic of Christ's teachings and his way of the cross. (Hershberger, B, 104-5)

The Dualism of Mennonite Pacifism. In his keen ability to interpret the traditional Mennonite peace position, J. H. Yoder asserts that "except within a nonresistant separated church, there is no foundation at all for nonresistance [and that] in some sense at least war is 'right for the government although it is wrong for us' " (Yoder, E, 109, quoting D. Smucker, 81). As the Schleitheim articles of the sixteenth-century confession of faith put it, the state is ordained of God "outside of the perfection of Christ" to maintain order through the use of the "sword" (i.e., police, jails, armies) (Yoder, G, 39). For Christians, of course, such forms of coercion are contrary to strict New Testament standards, while according to Romans 13, God mandated government for the restraint of all who do not live by New Testament principles.

This temptation to dualism was favored in addition by the cultural accommodation through which American Mennonites had gone in the last few generations. If one limits nonresistance to oneself, one can then be nonresistant and still patriotic and anti-communist; one can be accepted within denominational pluralism and within patriotic small-town society without representing a challenge. (Yoder, E, 109-10)

Gauging Traditional Mennonite Pacifism

In the CMP research project, six questions designed to test the adherence of Mennonites and Brethren in Christ to their traditional peace position were combined into a composite pacifism scale. Contrary to what we might have expected, members of liberal-type and transformist-type churches scored significantly higher on the scale than members of separatist and conservative churches. Responses to one of the questions show that barely half of our members from conservative churches agree with the statement, that "the Christian should take no part in war or any war-promoting activities," compared to 75% from liberal and transformist churches.

This reveals considerable separatist/conservative ambivalence about so-called conscientious objection to war. And as we will see below, the conservatives are even less interested in the newer forms of peacemaking initiative. Perhaps the conservatives think of pacifism as a liberal-type commitment, and they think of anything liberal as questionable.

Although about two-thirds of our respondents overall believe that Christians should take no part in war, about four out of ten of the separatist members (38%) and conservative members (40%) believe that the national government should take every opportunity, including military force, to stamp out communism at home and abroad. This documents the dualism in Yoder's interpretation of traditional Mennonite pacifism. Many Mennonites believe that God sanctions a particular military action even when they themselves cannot participate in it (Sider, 228).

Assertive Mennonite Peacemaking

The traditional dualist style of pacifism is a problem for more progressive and radical members of historic peace churches. "Those who teach the nonresistant way often translate pacifism (peacemaking) as passivism. They stress the command to 'resist not evil' and neglect the call to 'overcome evil with good.' They lack a sense of mission to the structures and powers of the world" (D. Brown, 44).

More assertive Mennonite peacemakers reinterpret the way of the cross in the perspective of Paul's teaching about the ministry of reconciliation (2 Cor. 5:16-19). In light of Paul's triumphant proclamation, nonresistance is certainly more than the refusal to participate in war or to serve in the armed forces of one's country. Nonresistance is a positive, transformationist ministry of reconciliation that has ethical relevance for all personal and social relationships.

> The emerging Mennonite position of recent decades affirms the lordship of Christ over all the "powers" of the cosmos as a basic theological premise. If Christ is indeed Lord over both church and world, then prophetic witness to the state is an integral part of the gospel message proclaiming the new age (J. R. Burkholder, 682).

The most historically obvious expression of traditional Mennonite pacifism has been an arrangement with the government whereby, in the face of a military draft, Mennonites could buy exemption. Exemptions have involved a commutation fee (Revolutionary War), hiring a substitute (Civil War), or being " assigned to work of national importance under civilian direction" (World War II).

Although Mennonites generally recognized that civilian public service was a more constructive provision for conscientious objectors than the prior arrangements, there was considerable post-World War II review of the ethic of love and nonresistance in light of Paul's teaching about the ministry of reconciliation.

> Many felt that from the point of view of the government, the purpose of CPS was primarily to keep the COs quiet and hidden away where they could not make an impression upon public opinion. Certainly this was one reason why Congress denied them the right to serve in foreign relief work, and certainly it was one of the reasons they were kept out of certain other positions where their example and teaching could have influenced American youth. . . .
>
> Some CPS men questioned whether they were not conscience-bound to protest this arrangement which to a certain degree forced their light under a bushel. They felt it was their duty to proclaim the message of peace everywhere and therefore they looked upon their assignments to isolated mountain camps as primarily designed to restrict their influence rather than to give them the opportunity to render the greatest possible service to their country and humanity. (Gingerich, 401-402)

This statement indicates the new distinction between traditional Mennonite conscientious objection and bolder forms of peacemaking. Nonregistration and other forms of civil disobedience were more frequently mentioned as alternatives to accepting a restrictive CO status.

Another bolder form of peace witness has been the refusal to pay war taxes.

> The war tax issue remained largely dormant during World War II. The first Mennonite to mention the subject was Austin Regier, a non-registrant who

was sentenced to a federal penitentiary for refusing to comply with the draft. He firmly believed that "the consistent pacifist would refuse war taxes." The idea of organizing war tax resistance in the United States seems to have begun with the Peacemaker Movement, which was formed by a heterogeneous group of pacifists in Chicago early in 1948. (D. Kaufman, 873-874)

The war tax issue has been more controversial in the churches than nonregistration. While the New Testament contains no sanction for Christians to perform military service, it does admonish them to pay their taxes (Mark 12:13-17, Rom. 13:6-7). In an article entitled, "Why I Don't Pay All of My Income Tax," published jointly in the *Gospel Herald* (MC) and *The Mennonite* (GCM), Yoder wrote that

> I want to pay my taxes and to pay them willingly as far as the functions of the United States government resemble what Jesus and Paul were talking about. The lesson of the entire New Testament is that Christians should be subject to political authority because in the providence of God the function of these authorities is to maintain peace. This is what I, in accordance with the instruction of the New Testament, am asking the American government to do. I am in fact even willing to pay for a certain amount of waste and fraud and incompetence, as well as for welfare service going beyond what Jesus and the apostles had in mind. But the one thing I am not prepared to support voluntarily is something which Jesus and Paul did not have in mind because it did not exist in the time of the New Testament. The government of Rome was not spending more than half of its resources to destroy the rest of the world. (Yoder, J, 81, 92)

The result of testimonies of peace activists like Regier and Yoder has been a new quest for more relevant and effective forms of peacemaking. Three subsequent developments will be highlighted here.

The first is a movement called the "New Call to Peacemaking." This was a coalition of Mennonites, Brethren, and Quakers that took form in 1977 to explore their common pacifist commitments, reexamine the biblical bases of peacemaking, and launch a more active peace witness.

> Numerous regional meetings between the three historic peace churches culminated in a national conference at Green Lake, Wis., in 1978. Two more national conferences followed in 1980 and 1982. With part-time staff and occasional steering committee meetings, "New Call" continues to sponsor publications and gatherings that seek both to meet needs within the peace church constituency and to promote peace activity among other Christians. (J. R. Burkholder, 684)

A second new movement is that of "Christian Peacemaker Teams." This program was the fruit of the spirited call by Ronald Sider, Brethren in Christ ethicist (currently member of a Mennonite church), to a costly kind of peacemaking in an address to the 1984 Mennonite World Conference in Strasbourg, France. Sider believes that the traditional Mennonite/BIC peace position has been weakened by serious misunderstandings of the biblical message. It has been isolationist, silent, uninvolved, negative, inconsistent, cowardly, and protective of Mennonite/BIC economic affluence.

Sider believes, moreover, that Jesus fulfilled his divine destiny as the suffering servant Savior of the world to bring to fulfillment the biblical vision of peace conveyed in the Hebrew word *shalom*—right relationships in every area of life.

> Jesus' approach to peacemaking was not to lapse into passive nonresistance; it was not to withdraw to isolated solitude; it was not to teach one ethic for the private sphere and another for public life. Jesus modeled an activist challenge to the status quo, summoning the entire Jewish people to accept his nonviolent messianic strategy instead of the Zealot's militaristic methods. (R. Sider, 234)

Sider's vision took root. After a study process in numerous congregations, a special consultation was held in 1986 in Illinois. Sider's concept of Christian peacemaking teams was endorsed and the call issued for the development of a recruitment and training program. The intent would be to prepare peacemaking teams to go intervene in conflict situations around the world "to reduce violence and foster justice through nonviolent action" (J. R. Burkholder, 684). Four denominations—Mennonite Church, General Conference Mennonite Church, Brethren in Christ, and Church of the Brethren—established a CPT steering committee which began meeting in 1987 to implement Sider's call for new approaches to peacemaking.

A third set of initiatives in peacemaking has developed out of the work of the Mennonite Central Committee—establishing Mennonite Conciliation Service; setting up lobbying offices in the national capitols of Washington and Ottawa; and organizing the MCC Peace Section, which functions as an ongoing think tank and disseminator of position statements on issues like the Persian Gulf War.

In congregations still committed to the more traditional isolationist style of pacifism, these newer peacemaking approaches have been controversial. "The constituent members of MCC have not come to full agreement on whether or not Mennonites should be involved in influencing legislation and government programs except when it directly affects the rights of Mennonites to practice their religious convictions" (Keeney, 686).

Gauging New Mennonite Peacemaking Initiatives

Indicators of these newer forms of peacemaking initiatives were included in the CMP II questionnaire. Again we found significant differences between our four church types, mainly between the conservative/ separatist churches and the liberal/transformist churches. The latter were more open to active promotion of the Mennonite/BIC peace position, a noncooperative attitude toward a military draft, nonpayment of war taxes, nonpurchase of stock in industries producing military hardware, and support of MCC offices in our national capitols to press the church's concerns about war and peace and other social justice matters.

This diversity of attitudes certainly came out in oral interviews with CMP respondents.

Glenn Klassen, conservative. Of all the things my parents taught me, one of the few things I rejected was when I joined the National Guard instead of registering as a conscientious objector. All of my younger brothers were in I-W work, but I couldn't do it. It's odd that now they're not attending church at all and I am.

It's odd also that after listening to Jerry Falwell for the past couple of years, my dad doesn't believe in conscientious objection anymore either, just as I'm having second thoughts about the military side. The MBs have a lot of rethinking to do on this issue.

With me it was peer pressure and hardly any peer support for pacifism. The CO label was the thing that gave Mennonite kids so much trouble. You wouldn't believe the names we got called in school. At that time I just couldn't take it. I'm still not sure I can say I'm an absolute pacifist, but I think I'd be open to a more active peace witness if the church really got serious about it.

Menno Isaac, transformist. Every war has such horrible excesses committed on both sides that the just war argument collapses. For me, and I think for everyone in our Fellowship, the idea of militarism as a nation's way to preserve peace is ludicrous. It may seem to work in the short run, but it inevitably fails in the long run.

Apart from the question of whether militarism is good for anything except that it gives jobs to a lot of people, we base our pacifism in the "power of the resurrection" referred to in Philippians 3:10. We have tried to imagine that future resurrection kingdom when violence of all kinds will be rendered dysfunctional, and when the pursuing forces of evil continue to try to attack with their weapons of violence, and our resurrection bodies are finally invulnerable.

Their swords pierce our bodies, their missiles pierce our aircraft, but no harm results because we finally live in spiritual bodies and fly in spiritual airplanes. Living in the power of the resurrection is not just for some future realm. We live and act now in the power of the resurrection and call all peoples and nations to do likewise. But we have an awful lot of discerning to do about what this means for our practical peacemaking.

How Congregations Can
Get Involved in Peacemaking

There is a serious gap between the self-identity of Mennonites/BICs as historic peace churches and the actual involvement of members in peace witness. For instance, 11% of our CMP respondents as a whole agree that a member of our churches ought not pay the proportion of income taxes that goes for military purposes. But only 3% have ever actually withheld any federal taxes proportionate to government military expenditures. Again, 62% of our CMP members (in 1972) believe that all young persons in our churches should devote a couple of years to some type of voluntary service, whether or not they face military draft. But in fact only 6% (by 1989) had ever done any voluntary service of at least one year duration.

The problem with Sider's vision for Christian Peacemaking Teams and his call for thousands to go to trouble spots of the world and die if necessary is its sense of unreality. Indeed, in November of 1990, a Christian Peacemaking Team actually went to Baghdad, Iraq, on a mission of peace. The team included eight Mennonites, two Brethren, one Brethren in Christ, and one Quaker (Garber, 10, 12-15).

They sought to listen to people there, to engage in any possible efforts to encourage peace, and to deliver medicines that were in short supply because of the economic embargo. While this effort did not avert the Persian Gulf War, the team was able to meet with high-level Iraqi government leaders and assure them that many Christians in the West supported a negotiated settlement of the Middle East crisis.

But the usual format of these meetings with officials was that they were ushered into a room to hear a long party-line speech while video cameras recorded every comment and person present. Most of the peacemaking team members were church leaders who could go without jeopardizing their jobs at home.

But what about rank-and-file members of our churches at home? How do they get involved in middle-range peacemaking efforts where they live and work? One of the best answers comes from a member of the Mennonite Brethren Church. With funds from the MCC Peace Section (U.S.), Mark Siemens spent the summer of 1983 visiting congregations that have implemented effective local peace ministries. Out of the experiences of these churches, Siemens developed a twenty-one point process of planning and implementing a congregational peace ministry.

The most important stage in the Siemens plan is the study and prayer sessions at the beginning of the process. For this the congregation needs several simple, short, well-written study guides to help members get a sound biblical foundation for Christian peacemaking (Siemens, 2-5).

But the Old Testament, with its long history of the wars of Israel, also raises the troublesome issue of God's apparent approval of violence and bloodshed. Mennonite thinkers have taken at least three approaches in responding to this problem. (1) The simplest is based on the words of Jesus that divide history into two epochs: "You have heard . . . but I say to you" [Matt. 5:21-43]. Whatever may have been commanded by Yahweh in the old dispensation is now superseded by the new way of Jesus. (2) G. F. Hershberger, concerned to find a more consistent understanding of the divine will, wrote of God's "concession to disobedience." Because the people of Israel were not faithful to God's high calling, they were consigned to live on the lower level of warfare and bloodshed. (3) More careful attention to the unique characteristics of biblical "holy war," at first glance a troublesome issue for peace theology, has revealed a theological model that minimizes human engagement in warfare as it calls for total trust and obedience to Yahweh, the transcendent warrior-king [Exod. 15:1-13]. (J. R. Burkholder, 682)

Related to the third approach is an excellent study book, Lois Barrett's *The Way God Fights* (Scottdale, Pa.: Herald Press, 1987). Although this book deals mostly with the issues of war and peace in the Old Testament, the last three chapters are on the concept of holy war in the New Testament.

Two additional study books written with denominational perspectives are Dale Brown's *Biblical Pacifism: A Peace Church Perspective* (Elgin, Ill.: Brethren Press, 1986) and the volume edited by John E. Toews and Gordon Nickel, *The Power of the Lamb* (Winnipeg, Man., and Hillsboro, Kan.: Kindred Press, 1986). The two books combine the transcendent vision of the Quakers with the sober realistic Mennonite commitment to nonresistance and our Lord's way of the cross in discipleship and peacemaking. In that blend are vital clues to how Christians can be peacemakers in these violent times.

Discussion Questions

1. Is pacifism the same thing as peacemaking? What are some different nuances of the two words in everyday language?

2. What are the main differences in the pacifist styles of Mennonites, Quakers, and Brethren? How would you account for these differences? Should the best elements of the three groups be blended into some new peacemaking initiatives?

3. The traditional Mennonite peace position has been transmitted from generation to generation for several centuries. How do you explain this continuity? Is it the result of a cultural characteristic of "the quiet in the land"? Or is it the product of a carefully crafted religious ethic? What are the pros and cons of the traditional Mennonite pacifist style?

4. In your experience, are Mennonites accurately described by the German word *Gelassenheit*, meaning peaceableness?

5. Which of the newer Mennonite peacemaking initiatives do you feel has the best chance of making an impact in the world: noncooperation with conscription laws, nonpayment of war taxes, "New Call to Peacemaking," "Christian Peacemaker Teams," peace witness through the Mennonite Central Committee?

6. Can you envision the God of Abraham, Isaac, Jacob, and Jesus as a warrior (Exod. 15:1-13)? What does this mean?

7. Would you like to see your congregation develop a special peacemaking witness?

CHAPTER 12

How Can Christians Make Political Decisions?

*Let every person be subject to
the governing authorities.*
—Romans 13:1

IN THE SPRING OF 1873, the Mennonite communities of South Russia sent delegates to Canada and the United States to "spy out the promised land" for prospective emigrants. Guided by a Canadian government official, a representative of the Ontario Mennonites, a representative of the Indiana Mennonites, and several railroad officials, the delegates toured Ontario, Manitoba, the Dakotas, Minnesota, Nebraska, Colorado, Kansas, and Texas.

The Mennonites had mandates from their home communities to learn what "privileges" they would be guaranteed in North America to compare with the privileges in Russia, now revoked, which had been granted them when they immigrated from West Prussia. These privileges had included exemption from military service, land of good quality at moderate prices on easy terms, and the right to live in separate self-administered, German-speaking communities.

The Canadian official agreed to such privileges. But replies from the U.S. officials had to be processed at the highest levels of government—the Congress of the United States and the president himself, including his secretaries of state and the interior. President Ulysses S. Grant, a Civil War general, wanted to be helpful to the Russian Mennonites and mentioned this in his 1874 state of the union address to Congress. However, a more cautious secretary of state, Hamilton Fish, admonished the president to be realistic.

> I fear that even the qualified . . . answer which you propose should be given is one that circumstances may prove not capable of the certainty of real-

156

ization and that should this large and interesting community . . . make the sacrifices which they picture with much feeling, of leaving their homes and their "cherished memories" and incur the large pecuniary loss which they must incur, and then within the fifty years of the future which no one can foreshadow find the necessities of a war calling upon them for commutations, and finding as they must find the state laws imposing military and jury duty and interfering with their schools, they will imagine that the hope held out to them has proved delusive. (L. Harder, A, 55-56)

Although the Russian Mennonite delegates did not obtain the guaranteed privileges they desired, they certainly got a new impression of how a democracy works in contrast to a monarchy like Tsarist Russia. This reassured them that life in America without the specific privileges requested would be preferable to the loss of privileges in Russia.

On their way home several of the Mennonite delegates met personally with President Grant. They were served a glass of wine as they waited to see the President. Peter Janzen wrote that

in Russia we associated a government official with a uniform and lots of lace and trimmings, and the higher ones would always have guards of soldiers at the entrances to their quarters and residences. Imagine our surprise when we reached the White House to find the portals guarded by a single colored man who not even displayed a sword. (Janzen, 35)

As long as their host country gave them relative autonomy and exemption from military service, Mennonites were content to live under authoritarian or democratic governments. In return they pledged obedience to the existing norms of law and order, in keeping with Romans 13:1. In whatever the political environment, their traditional attitude toward government was separatist and largely nonpolitical.

In Europe through the centuries, this attitude was largely conditioned by low toleration for their minority Anabaptist faith. In Russia, their patriotism kept more than half of the Mennonites from trying to emigrate until their very survival was threatened after the Russian Revolution, and then for many it was too late to leave.

Those who managed to get out and immigrate to North America came with a new aversion to anarchy and communist totalitarianism and a new appreciation for the freedoms of democratic government. In North America their traditional stance of withdrawal was bound sooner or later to come under criticism from within as well as from without. With new freedoms they had hardly experienced before came new questions about their civic responsibilities and their Christian duty to bear witness to the evangelical and ethical dimensions of their faith.

Responses to these kinds of political questions in the CMP research project represented three general attitudes or positions about participa-

tion in politics—nonparticipation, full participation, and selective participation.

Nonparticipation in Politics. All five denominations have histories reflecting apolitical attitudes. Before the turn of the century, members of
the Franconia Conference (MC) were admonished by their elders "not to
accept any public office [and] it is considered advisable to abstain from
voting" (Wenger, 53-55, 443). This ruling was reaffirmed as late as 1933
in a reissuance of the "Rules and Discipline of the Franconia Conference
of the Mennonite Church."

The minutes of the Brethren in Christ General Conferences from
1871 to 1904 contained similar prohibitions, for instance,

> Inasmuch as we believe that there is a great danger in opening the door for
> brethren to hold public offices indiscriminately . . . we would advise that
> brethren should not allow themselves to be used in public offices for fear of
> becoming involved in political strife, which is contrary to the faith of the
> church on conscientious principles." (BIC, 72)

In the same vein, an 1878 conference resolution of the Mennonite
Brethren Church ruled that "members are not permitted to hold government offices or take any part at the polls." This wording was followed by
the interesting afterthought anticipating the criticisms that were bound
to come: "However, we appreciate the protection we enjoy under our
government" (Redekop, C, 95). Already by 1890 this ruling was softened
a little, partly for obvious pragmatic reasons: "Members of the church
should refrain from participation or involvement in the contentions of
political parties but are permitted to vote quietly at elections *and may also
vote for prohibition*" (Redekop, C, 95; italics added).

The attitude of nonparticipation is still measurable in the churches,
especially those with MC affiliation. The 1946 Mennonite Confession of
Faith reiterated the traditional dualism of the MC political ethic.

> In law enforcement the state does not and cannot operate on the nonresis-
> tance principles of Christ's kingdom. Therefore, nonresistant Christians
> cannot undertake any service in the state or in society which would violate
> the principles of love and holiness as taught by Christ and his inspired
> apostles. (MCF, 54)

Full Participation in Politics. The opposite attitude approves free participation in the political realm while holding to the pacifist commitment in
principle. This kind of "freedom in nonessentials" has characterized the
GCMC throughout its history and the EMC after World War II. "The
GCMC has adopted no official position on the subject and typically assumes that each member is competent and responsible to make his [or

her] own decisions concerning political participation" (Kauffman/Harder, 154).

The argument for full participation was expressed by J. Winfield Fretz.

> If one carefully examines the logic of nonparticipation in a political democracy, one is forced to the position of abandoning political rule to the evil and the unprincipled and the unscrupulous. Naturally, if the righteous withdraw from participation, only the unrighteous are left. How then can pure, honest, wise, creative government be expected to result? If the logic of the Mennonites were to be followed by all Christians everywhere, it would mean that no Christians would be willing to hold public offices. Hence Christians who believed in voting would have to vote for non-Christians only. This type of ascetic withdrawal from assuming full responsibility for the social order in which we live seems to me unrealistic, unwise, and in a sense less than courageously Christian. . . .
>
> It is becoming increasingly clear to me that the traditional Mennonite attitude toward political nonparticipation is untenable in the kind of political system under which we live. Not only is it possible for a Christian to hold public office and be a dedicated Christian, it is the duty of consecrated Christians to hold public office and thus serve both God and man. (Fretz, 144)

John Redekop compiled a four-page listing of Mennonites who have run for political office on the national and state/provincial levels of government in Canada and the United States, most of them members of the GCMC (Redekop, C, 96-9). James Juhnke observes that

> Since World War II Mennonites in the five western provinces of Canada became more extensively involved as voters and as officeholders in provincial and national politics than Mennonites have ever been anywhere. In recent elections from three to ten Mennonites have stood for provincial offices while fifteen or more have been nominated for national offices. Canadian Mennonite politicians have belonged to many different political parties and have expressed widely varying political views, including positions on military defense which are in tension with Mennonite pacifist teachings. (Juhnke, A, 710-11)

Indeed some Mennonite congregations not only endorse full participation in politics but also no longer rule out police and military roles for their members.

Selective Participation in Politics. Other Mennonite ethicists reject both options of nonparticipation and uncritical participation.

> What mattered more to the early Christians was another set of questions, namely, who their Lord should be if it was not Caesar, and what kind of life he asked of them. . . . They were oriented to another Lord. Their faithfulness to that Lord led them to tolerate Caesar on one level and to disobey

him on others. . . . Caesar is thus not the point of their orientation so that one could say to him either yes or no. Both the "relevance" people today who call for us to plunge into the public arena, the way it is structured, by choosing the best of the available partisan options, and the "withdrawal" people, who call upon us to protect the purity of our irrelevance, make the assumption that you can say systematically either "yes" or "no" to Caesar. . . .

[However] Caesar's world and the world of Christ are not separate compartments or separate worlds but intersecting paths through the same terrain. They deal with the same questions, in the same time and space, but according to other points of orientation. . . . This then creates some possible common ground between the agenda of the kingdom of Christ and the agenda of Caesar's least tyrannical vision. . . . So it is that a society which has heard something of Christian witness, and has created room for less violent and more dialogical procedures in civil participation, has therefore created a space in which the disciples of Christ can participate civilly without denying their faith and without bearing the sword. (Yoder, H, 11-12)

Yoder's essay argues for what has been called selective participation in politics. Yoder accepts the obligation to be engaged in the political sphere to the extent that opportunity presents and conscience is not violated while maintaining a prior orientation to the lordship of Christ. The crucial element in this position, according to Elmer Ediger, is to discern the points of engagement and the points of withdrawal.

Although this . . . point of view would readily agree that we must shift to a positive emphasis toward greater political participation, this view would also underscore the Christian's larger mission and the necessity that every Christian in politics have a point of withdrawal. Rather than being forced into a position of directly doing that which he [or she] as a Christian considers wrong, a Christian disciple withdraws with a witness to be relevant in a higher Christian sense. . . . Though different from much in recent Mennonite tradition, this view nevertheless feels akin to early Anabaptism in that this is a narrow path of discipleship which is in the world but not of it. (E. Ediger, 144)

The only CMP-participant denomination that has officially endorsed this third position is the Mennonite Brethren Church. In 1978, its General Conference adopted a resolution stating that "the Christian church has been given a mandate to bring Christian concerns to bear in all situations. . . . For faithful Christians an acknowledgment of this mandate . . . requires cautious, *selective involvement in the political realm*" (MBC, 24).

The resolution contained the admonitions to pray for those in positions of political authority, to become informed about the political situation, to vote in public elections, to communicate their individual and collective views to government officials, and to stand for political office when a member feels called to do so and insofar as it does not compromise Christian ethics.

Gauging Attitudes Toward Political Participation

The CMP research project used various indicators of political participation. Overall, about 10% of the members of the five participant denominations still adhere to the absolute political nonparticipation position—which involves believing that members should not vote, hold government office, witness directly to the state, or try to influence government on social issues. Conversely, by these same indicators about 90% affirm either full or selective participation.

The conservative congregations have larger proportions of members who adhere to the nonparticipation position (about 17% for separatist and 11% for conservative churches) than have the liberal types (7% for liberal and 9% for transformist churches). Over 50% of all members voted in most or all of the recent public elections (although there is a difference of 24% between the separatist and liberal churches on this indicator).

Political Party Preferences

In Canada as well as in the United States, the voting decisions of Mennonites and Brethren in Christ are made with regard to political parties that seek to win control of the government in popular elections. John Redekop believes that

> there is no "one to one" correlation between Anabaptist Christianity and any political creed. . . . Individual Christians may decide to join a party and participate to one degree or another [but] they should be aware of the significance of their actions and must be very careful not to weaken or undermine the church by attempting to tie it closely to any political creed, party or country." (Redekop, B, 12)

Although both countries have mainly a two-party system, there are often smaller parties or factions within the same party trying to gain a foothold. This is especially true in Canada, where minority parties seem to have more chance to capture votes, depending on the issues at stake. One of the main parties generally represents a somewhat more conservative, and the other a more liberal point of view. At least in principle the parties represent political identification on a continuum from *conservatism* (the philosophy that wants to use government to preserve the values of the past) to *liberalism* (the philosophy that wants to use government to implement changes in relation to such social problems as unemployment, health care needs, and social-economic inequality).

In the United States, the two-party system came to prevail despite the hope of the founding fathers that the new government could operate without political parties. In modern times the Republican party has come to be seen as supporting conservative policies, with the Democrats tending toward more liberal policies (though Democrat Bill Clinton has tried to broaden the Democrats' image).

In view of the importance of political parties in the Canadian and American systems, we asked our respondents, "With which one of the following (American)(Canadian) political positions do you tend to be most in sympathy or agreement?" We found that U.S. Mennonites tend to be more politically neutral than Canadian Mennonites. In Canada only 14% of the members overall took no political party position, compared to 23% in the United States. Moreover, nearly half of the Canadian members preferred the Progressive Conservative party, and only 20% the Liberal party. The Conservative party was the preference in all four church types, although the members of the liberal churches were about equally divided between Conservative, Liberal, and one of the third party choices (NDP or Social Credit).

In the U.S. churches, members preferred the Republican party to the Democratic party on nearly a 3 to 1 ratio overall (more than 4 to 1 in the two conservative-type churches). Of those who expressed a party preference (omitting the neutral category), 70% chose the Republican party, 25% the Democratic party, and 4% preferred some other party or chose to remain independent.

Mennonite political observers have tried to understand why U.S. Mennonites and Brethren in Christ tend to prefer the Republican party. James Juhnke pointed to

> historical factors which fostered the Republican preference [such as] Mennonite opposition to slavery and to the Democrat South's Civil War rebellion against the national government (American Civil War), a positive response to generous Republican land policies on the frontier, and the concentration of Mennonite settlements in strongly Republican states." (Juhnke, A, 710)

Ted Koontz believes that "Mennonite voting patterns are heavily dependent on the social, economic, and political ethos of their communities. Thus in the United States *rural Mennonites* . . . tend to vote heavily for conservative Republican candidates" (Koontz, A, 159; italics added).

CMP data tend to confirm Koontz' hunch. Fifty-eight percent of the members whose place of residence is rural preferred the Republican party, compared to only 48% of members who live in small or large cities. Conversely, only 13% of the rural members prefer the Democratic party, compared to 25% who live in a small city and 35% who live in a large city.

On the educational factor (deleting those who take no political position at all), 83% of the members with no more than a high school diploma prefer the Republican party, while only 46% of the members who have gone to graduate school prefer the Republican party, the same percentage as those who prefer the Democratic party. Thus higher education is associated with liberal politics.

Among Canadian members, rural-urban place of residence and amount of schooling appear to have little relationship to choice of political party, or even to whether or not a political position is taken at all, except that members preferring the New Democratic Party tend to be more highly educated. Similarly, amount of income has no significant correlation with the party preference of Canadian members.

Among U.S. Mennonites, however, 65% of the members with annual household incomes over $50,000 prefer the Republican party compared with only 43% of members with less than $15,000 income. Moreover, 40% of the members with annual incomes of less than $15,000 take no political position at all, compared to only 14% of members with incomes over $50,000.

Koontz suspects that "some of this [party preference] may be explained by the influence of conservative radio and television preachers in parts of the Mennonite world" (Koontz, A, 161). In their analysis of our CMP II data, Kauffman and Driedger conclude that the political preferences of Mennonites and Brethren in Christ are among the most conservative of Protestant denominations (Kauffman/Driedger, 142). John Redekop critiques the political conservatism of Mennonites.

> Anabaptist conservative Christianity holds certain orientations in common with political conservatism—an emphasis on individualism and individual responsibility; a more or less pessimistic view of human nature (man is more evil than ignorant); rejection of a belief in natural and inevitable human progress and moral evolution; acceptance of a hierarchy of authority; acceptance of the view that majority decisions may not always be morally correct; and an agreement that philosophical absolutes are important.
>
> However, there are also important areas of tension between our Christian views and those of political conservatism. Quite logically, in our pluralistic society, political conservatives cannot ipso facto posit the Christian gospel as the cornerstone of their philosophy, platform or policies. Additionally, Anabaptist Christians, and all others who take seriously the transnational character of the church, have problems subscribing to commonplace conservative emphases on superpatriotism, militant nationalism, and the idea that private property is sacrosanct. Perhaps most important of all, Anabaptist Christians reject the conservative notion that the norm for human experience lies in human history, in the collective human experience. While acknowledging the importance of human experience, Christians look beyond it for the ultimate standard. (Redekop, B, 12)

Voting Behavior

The actual choices that our respondents make in the voting booth add a note of realism to the portrait already painted. Both in Canada and the United States, Mennonite and Brethren in Christ voters in 1988 threw their support to the Conservative and Republican candidates by a 14% higher margin than the national vote. Moreover, the members of the conservative-type of church voted for Mulroney and Bush by significantly greater percentages than did members of the liberal-type church.

Political Discernment in the Congregation

Do Mennonite and Brethren in Christ voters really discern the issues in light of Christian ethical principles when they go into the voting booths? A convincing answer to that question will not be given here except to introduce one more set of questions followed by some value judgments based on some principles of Christian political discernment.

The political discernment of church members can be and should be corporate as well as individual. To gauge attitudes about the role of the church in the political process, we asked our church members a series of four questions about the appropriate function of the congregation in an election year.

Do you feel it is proper for your congregation to

1. Encourage its members to study political issues and candidates?
2. Encourage its members to engage in political action?
3. Endorse particular candidates for office?
4. Encourage the minister to discuss political issues from the pulpit?

The questions covered a range from least to most congregational involvement in the political discernment process. Overall, there was a diminishing approval of the four kinds of congregational involvement. Seventy-nine percent approved the study of political issues and candidates but only 28% approved the minister's discussing political issues from the pulpit. Again the differences are significant, but here the members of the two separationist-type churches (separatist and transformist) were closer together in resisting congregational involvement in these ways while the members of the two integrationist-type churches (conservative and liberal) more readily approved it.

How Can Christ Be Lord of Our Politics?

The confession of the early church, "Jesus Christ is Lord," is basic to the faith of Christians of every generation. By making this confession Christians commit themselves to follow him as Lord in all areas of their lives—personal and social, religious and secular, economic and political. But how can Christ be Lord of our politics?

In 1980, while pastoring the St. Louis Mennonite Fellowship (a transformist-type church) the writer received a letter with enclosures from Daniel Kauffman, then pastor of the Mt. Pisgah Mennonite Church near Leonard, Missouri. He asked the members of the St. Louis Fellowship to go to the polls that November to vote against an amendment allowing bingo gambling in the state. Despite the fact that Dan's parents probably had biblical reasons why Mennonites should not register and vote, most members of the Fellowship agreed with him that it was their privilege and duty to vote. They needed to vote their convictions on moral issues like this and not to leave the political decision making to unbelievers.

But as Dan's letter was discussed, some of our members were less certain that it was the Christian's responsibility to keep people from gambling their money on bingo, to legislate in the moral realm, and to try to make things come out right in the public sphere. They felt that this is what the separation of church and state was all about. As members of Christ's church, their first duty was to an alternate political order, the kingdom of God. The commission is to call men and women to get out of certain demonic structures (like bingo parlors?) into God's kingdom, rather than to try by legislation and law enforcement to control or constrain such structures for the glory of God.

This was the basic difference, they felt, between the state churches of the sixteenth century and the Anabaptists. Nevertheless, the Fellowship agreed that they would vote in the election if qualified and would vote against the amendment, together with the members of the Mt. Pisgah Church. The significance of this decision was less the specific issue at stake than the consensus that as Mennonite congregations we had a responsibility to discern the issues under the lordship of Christ and give counsel and advice to each other.

We found help that year in a pamphlet entitled, *Can My Vote Be Biblical?* published by Evangelicals for Social Action. The pamphlet began with nine basic biblical principles.

1. The family is a divinely willed institution.
2. Every human life is sacred.
3. Religious and political freedom are God-given, inalienable rights.
4. God and his people have a very special concern for the poor.
5. God requires just economic patterns in society.
6. God requires Christians to be peacemakers.
7. The Creator requires stewardship of the earth's resources.
8. Sin is both personal and social.
9. Personal integrity is vital. (ESA)

To follow Christ's lordship in the voting booth means to evaluate issues and candidates by their adherence to such biblical principles as these. As Christians trying to make political decisions, we are interdependent with each other in the church and with knowledgeable and concerned people and groups in the larger community.

By using reliable guides to the political views and voting records of candidates, paying attention to their public statements, making personal contacts and asking pertinent questions, commissioning fact-finding committees in our church to provide guidance on election issues, and actively participating in political discernment groups in church and community, we can trust the Holy Spirit to guide our involvements at each level of government. In truth our political involvement is one of the crucial ways by which we bear witness that Jesus Christ is Lord indeed.

Discussion Questions

1. Why did Secretary of State Hamilton Fish not want to promise special privileges to the Mennonites? In your judgment, how have pacifist Mennonites and Brethren in Christ been treated in Canada and the U.S. with respect to their religious beliefs?

2. Do the members of our churches who still hold to a political non-participation position have a valid argument? If so, what is it? If not, why not?

3. Do you consider yourself a political conservative, a political liberal, or something else? Share your self-identities in this regard and discuss the pros and cons of political conservatism and political liberalism.

4. Do the political parties in Canada and the U.S. provide authentic options on the basis of principle? Or do they overlap so much that the differences are negligible?

5. To explain Mennonite and BIC political conservatism, Juhnke cites historical factors and Koontz points to sociological and religious factors. How would you explain the fact that Mennonites and BICs are among the most politically conservative of all North American Protestant groups?

6. How did you feel about the two Mennonite congregations in Missouri giving advice and counsel to each other as to how to vote on a particular issue (bingo gambling) in the election? Should the congregation give advice and counsel to its members in an election year?

CHAPTER 13

How Can We Discern Other Issues of Our Time?

Be transformed by the renewing of your minds,
so that you may discern what is the will of God.
—Romans 12:2

IN 1991 *The Day America Told the Truth,* a new book on American morality, was published by Prentice Hall Press. The book was alleged to be the most massive in-depth social-scientific survey of the moral attitudes and behavior of Americans ever conducted.

Following are some of the startling findings.

Nine out of ten respondents lie regularly. (Patterson/Kim, 45)

Nearly one-third of all married respondents have had an adulterous affair. (94)

Twenty-five percent of the respondents under 25 years of age lost their virginity by the age of 13, compared to 10% for ages 45-64 and 5% for ages 65 and older. (103)

Twenty percent of the female respondents say they have been date-raped (128), and less than 3% of date rapes are reported. (130)

One-third of the respondents own handguns (132), and for 10 million dollars, 7% say they would be willing to kill a stranger. (66)

Only one in ten believe in all of the Ten Commandments. (200)

Ninety percent say that they believe in God, but for most "religion plays virtually no role in shaping their opinions on a long list of important moral questions." (199)

Three of the 54 "revelations" from the survey listed in the last chapter are—

1. "At this time, America has no moral leadership. Americans believe, across the board, that our current political, religious, and business leaders have failed us." (235)

2. "Americans are making up their own rules and laws. . . . There is absolutely no moral consensus in this country—as there was in the 1950s and 1960s." (235)

3. "The 1990s will be marked by very personalized moral crusades. Many of us ache to do the right thing, but we feel that there are no sane outlets through our institutions." (235-236)

In the face of this kind of massive data on the moral degeneracy of our culture, have Mennonite and Brethren in Christ churches also lost moral distinctiveness? Have we become conformists rather than dissenters representing a counter-culture "nonconformed to this world" (Rom. 12:2a)? Among the vast array of immoral influences bearing down upon us, are we also losing clarity on what is right and wrong, wholesome and unwholesome? Even more to the central point of our book, have we lost the high calling of the gospel to be transformed by the renewing of our minds, so we may discern what is the will of God—what is good and acceptable and perfect (Rom. 12:2)?

The Mennonite/BIC
Context for Moral Discernment

Throughout their history, Mennonites and Brethren in Christ have listed holy living as a mark by which their authenticity as a church was to be gauged. They called their members to a moral nonconformity "visible in that these people keep their promises, love their enemies, enjoy their neighbors, and tell the truth, as others do not" (Yoder, C, 263-264).

Today as never before, seeking consensus on the controversial moral issues of our time is fraught with tension between traditionalists, who see things as stark right or wrong choices, and relativists who see more ambiguities. When churches try to focus on the biblical and pastoral questions raised by such issues, the debate often alienates and polarizes members instead of leading to redemptive communication and understanding.

The moral traditionalists tend to be hardliners, asserting standards of right and wrong with dogmatic certainty (Bellah, 140). The moral relativists who want to remain open-minded on all issues and hear all points of view tend to defer judgment indefinitely, unwittingly reinforcing the attitude of permissiveness in our society that tolerates moral license. As Kauffman and Driedger observe,

> consensus can never be reached if closure is indefinitely postponed. Hence many church members, impatient with those who would debate issues endlessly, seek a "word from the Lord" or from church leaders that will end the arguments and provide a solid basis from which there can be forward movement in Christian education and righteous living. (Kauffman/ Driedger, 187)

Many moral traditionalists in Mennonite and BIC churches believe that so much discussion on issues like abortion, capital punishment, and homosexuality is itself a sign that we are being unduly influenced by our culture. This attitude fails to recognize that there has never been a time when the norms taught us by our forebears did not need reinterpreting in the face of new experiences and influences. The dietary norms of the Old Testament had to be reinterpreted in New Testament churches. And when Mennonites wanted to attend the World's Fair in Chicago in 1892, their leaders had to reinterpret the norm of nonconformity to the world. It was not enough to assert, as one bishop tried, that "this is the *world's* fair, for the world and not for the Christian" (Juhnke, C, 21-27).

Mennonite and BIC readers can glean considerable reassurance from CMP findings. The survey shows that on a wide range of moral attitudes and behavior on which there are fairly clear Christian norms, CMP respondents scored significantly higher than the general population and members of other denominations. The comparisons, however, and especially the trends within our churches toward greater permissiveness in some areas and greater restrictiveness in others, warrant ongoing study and review.

The Issue of Abortion

Since the 1973 U.S. Supreme Court Roe vs. Wade decision that no state may prevent a woman's right to obtain an abortion for any reason during the first trimester of pregnancy, there have been countless millions of abortions in America. Although a baby at seven months can be viable outside of the womb, some states allow second and third trimester abortions. These developments have created a polarization of attitudes in which approximately 48% of the general population is in favor of the Court's decision, 48% opposed, and 4% uncertain.

Increasingly Mennonite and BIC congregations have to face the issue one way or another when members are making decisions about whether or not to terminate unwanted pregnancies. They know that what is lawful is not necessarily moral. For some members and congregations, the issue is whether or not to identify publicly with the pro-life or pro-choice activists who are lobbying to support or overturn the Court's decision. For more of them, the issue is whether for Christians abortion is ever permissible—and if so under what conditions.

Both the 1972 and 1989 CMP questionnaires asked respondents whether they believed that it should be possible for a pregnant woman to obtain a legal abortion for any of six reasons.

1. There is a strong chance of serious defect in the baby.
2. The woman's health is seriously endangered by the pregnancy.
3. The family has a very low income and cannot afford more children.
4. She became pregnant as a result of rape.
5. She is not married and does not want to marry the man.
6. She does not want the baby.

Persons selected one of three responses to each reason: yes, no, or uncertain. Out of a total of 17,251 responses to all six items in the 1989 survey, 21% were yes, 61% were no, and 18% were uncertain. Although 85% of Mennonite and BIC respondents believe abortion is not always wrong, the only circumstance for which this percentage applies is the endangerment of the woman's health. Even for this circumstance, the approving percentage was 7 percentage points more restrictive in 1989 than in 1972. Moreover, when we compared our respondents to North Americans generally, we observed that Mennonites and BICs are significantly more opposed to legalized abortion than the general population.

Despite the pro-life attitude among Mennonites and BICs as a whole, there is a significant attitudinal difference between our four types of church. On our composite abortion scale, scored somewhat differently (see Kauffman-Driedger, 196), the percentages of members opposed to abortion *for any reason* are 34, 21, 20, and 12 for separatist, conservative, transformist, and liberal churches, respectively. However, the percentages in the middle according to this scale are 56, 52, 60, and 49 for the same churches. Over half the members seem to vacillate on this issue from "no" on one reason for abortion to "yes" on another. The kinds of opinions held by the members are represented in our interviews with CMP respondents.

> *Sally Mae Stauffer, separatist.* I have to uphold God's law, "Thou shalt not kill." According to God's law, to willfully destroy the life in the womb is murder. We cannot leave God out of this abortion question. We belong to him. He is our Creator. The direct killing of an unborn for any reason is against the fifth commandment.
>
> *Glenn Klassen, conservative.* You hear women today say they have a right over their own bodies. The truth is that none of us has an absolute right over anything that God has created, least of all over the human body, which Paul called "the temple of God" [1 Cor. 3:16-17]. But I also don't think that the government has a right to legislate the decision either. If we really believe in separation of church and state, let's keep the government out of it.
>
> *Denise Preheim, liberal.* I'm inherently distrustful of any argument that promotes either pro-choice or pro-life at any cost. With babies being aborted in the second and third trimester of pregnancy, I find it unthinkable that the pro-choice people would champion abortion at any cost.
>
> On the other side, pro-life at any cost means that women who are victims of rape or incest would be forced to carry their babies to full term. I think that's wrong.

Another fundamental mistake of the pro-life people is that they have forgotten that there is life after birth. They never mention the impossible social environments that so many of these babies are born into. For children forced to grow up in violent, abusive, drug-infested, and crime-ridden homes and neighborhoods, it might have been better had they never been born [Mark 14:21].

Menno Isaac, transformist. The issue turns on the question of when life begins—at conception or birth? Those who say at birth define life as essentially the infant's ability to survive outside of the womb. I believe life begins at the moment of conception, when a new and unique human being is created with his or her own genetic code by which a whole human body develops from that single beginning cell. The abortion of that creation at any point along the way is fundamentally wrong, although there may be some mitigating factors like threat to the survival of the mother.

Leroy Walters, a BIC ethicist, distinguishes between three attitudes on this issue: restrictive, liberal, and mediating. Walters discusses the strengths and weaknesses of each position (an excellent resource for congregations studying this issue).

The restrictive position argues that abortion is not permissible under any circumstances. The proponent of this position says an absolute no to abortion, just as the pacifist says an absolute no to war. . . .

[The liberal position argues that] a pregnant woman has an absolute right to determine whether or not she will bear her child. . . .

[The mediating position] attempts to take account of a plurality of values, rather than according absolute value either to fetal life or to the desire of the woman. It inevitably involves the decision-maker in a complex process of drawing lines or weighing various factors. (Walters, 43-49)

Unlike the issues of capital punishment and homosexuality, discussed below, no Scripture references refer to abortion as such, which is "an issue not faced then but being faced now," as we put it in the last section of chapter 10. This is not to say that biblical texts cannot be used in the discernment process, but that members should beware of naive prooftexting.

For instance, Christian pro-life activists have cited Proverbs 24:11-12, "If you hold back from rescuing those taken away to death . . . does not he who keeps watch over your soul know it?" This text refers to oppressed peoples who are unjustly condemned to death. It takes a stretch of the imagination to apply it to unborn fetuses, as does the pro-life organization Operation Rescue.

Christian pro-choice activists have quoted Mark 14:21b, "It would have been better for that one not to have been born," as though Jesus was talking about therapeutic abortion and not about the betrayal of Judas.

Despite the complexities of the issue, Edwin and Helen Alderfer spoke the mind of a group of Mennonite and BIC persons attending a

Conference on abortion (sponsored by the Mennonite Medical Association) when they wrote the following direction for the future.

> We will see the importance of studying the question of abortion in our churches. Instead of taking the "easy road" of saying that a person should have the right to decide personally, the church will disengage itself from general society and say that it is a matter for a group of believers to discern the Spirit's leading, and they will pledge themselves to support the person or persons in need of their care. (Alderfer, 110)

The Issue of Capital Punishment

Capital punishment is an issue on which Mennonites and BICs are more evenly divided. In the CMP questionnaire, members were asked to respond to this statement: "Our national, provincial, or state governments should provide for capital punishment (the death penalty for a major crime)." Overall, 34% agreed, 40% disagreed, and a sizable 26% were undecided. Those approving of capital punishment increased by 4% since 1972. In the U.S., 68% of the people favor legal execution (Patterson/Kim, 177).

Again the responses varied significantly by type of church. On this issue, more of the members of separatist and conservative churches supported the death penalty (45% and 41%) in comparison to 19% and 26% for the liberal and transformist churches, with about a fourth of the members uncertain about this question. Elmer Martens, professor of Old Testament at the MB Biblical Seminary, summarizes the typical pro and con arguments.

Oppose

The stipulation of "life for life" [Exod. 21:24, Lev. 24:20, Deut. 19:21] was not enforced with Cain, the first murderer (Gen. 4:8-15), nor with David (2 Sam. 11:1—12:23). Jesus refused to advocate stoning for the woman caught in adultery (John 8:3-12), though biblical law so prescribed. The direction in the Bible, it is claimed, is from an older severity to a stance of grace, from retribution to rehabilitation. Genesis 9:6, which on the face of it calls for the death penalty for murderers, is explained

Approve

The Bible substantiates that the death penalty is a deterrent (Deut. 13:10-11). Capital punishment is not venting one's vengeance; there is a large difference between proper judicial process and revenge. As for cutting short the criminal's opportunity for repentance, the criminal, since he knows the time of his end, has greater reason for repentance. If the legal system is faulty and innocent people are consigned to execution, then the solution is not the abolition of the death penalty but the reform of the as being in the nature of an atonement. With Christ's satisfactory atonement, such demands fall away. The legal system is not foolproof, and innocent persons have been convicted and executed. Frequently, members of minority groups suffer the ultimate penalty, while wealthy or influential people do not. According to some sociological studies, the enforcement of capital punishment has not been a deterrent to crime. Life imprisonment, rather than the death penalty, is a more humane form of punishment. To cut short a criminal's life is to cut short the opportunity to repent. Psychologically, capital punishment is evil because it feeds the desire for revenge. The death penalty is a form of retaliation. Moreover, by putting the criminal to death, society commits the very evil it protests (ME, IV, 125).

legal system. Those who support capital punishment also stress the sacredness of life. It is precisely because men and women are made in God's image—a permanent factor in the creation order—that anyone taking human life forfeits his own right to life (Gen. 9:6). The directive in Genesis 9:6 has not an atonement context, but is intended to restrain disorder in society. Nor has this command been rescinded or revoked. Those who do wrong have reason to fear, for the governmental authority "does not bear the sword for nothing" (Rom. 13:4). Nor did Jesus' statement to the woman caught in adultery (John 8:3-12) set aside the death penalty. Had they indeed observed protocol, the accusers would have brought the male offender also, as the law stipulated (Lev. 20:10). (ME, IV, 125).

Is it conceivable that a local congregation can sort out these arguments, seeking the mind of Christ, and arrive at a consensus as Jesus mandated it to do (Matt. 8:18-20)?

The Unresolved Issue of Homosexuality

In one way or another, all of our four representative church members expressed attitudes against the practice of homosexuality. Two (Denise Preheim and Menno Isaac) would not bar homosexuals from church membership if they remained celibate. Menno admitted that

> this is a tough issue to discern, because no one in our Fellowship wants to be flippant about it, especially since we haven't yet had to face having a gay person in our group. I don't have the final answer on it, but my gut feeling is that it's wrong. Human anatomy was not intended for sexual intercourse between two males or two females. Even if someone has a disposition toward it, it's not right.
> We know the risks of disease and injury from such forced contact, and I'd have to assume that God did not design us to be that way. We hear and

read about all kinds of sexual perversions, and to me that's one of them. Granted that that's supposedly not like what a Christian homosexual relationship is like, I still don't feel it's right, unless they live together as friends and have a special love for each other, but not in a sexual way.

Homosexuality is an issue on which closure was theoretically reached in the General Conference Mennonite Church (1986, 81% majority vote) and in the Mennonite Church (1987, by consensus). Yet the issue appears not to have been fully resolved. Consequently, it provides interesting data for a case study with the purpose of discerning whether there is another way to work at various moral issues like this.

In nearly identical resolutions, the two delegate bodies declared that according to biblical teaching, "sexual intercourse is reserved for a man and a woman united in marriage," that "violation of this teaching is a sin," and that this teaching categorically "precludes premarital, extramarital, and homosexual sexual activity." However, the resolution also censured "our fear and . . . our rejection of those of us with a different sexual orientation and . . . our lack of compassion for their struggle to find a place in society and in the church." The resolution committed members and churches to remain "in loving dialogue with each other in the body of Christ" and acknowledged "that we are all sinners in need of God's grace and that the Holy Spirit may lead us to further truth and repentance" (HS, 165-168).

Meanwhile the Brethren/Mennonite Council for Lesbian and Gay Concerns (BMC), founded in 1976, is a growing gay activist movement. BMC is conspicuously present at every MC/GCMC General Assembly/ General Conference and on most of our college campuses, dispensing literature and conducting seminars.

Largely as a response to the persistent verbal BMC witness, the General Boards of the two Mennonite denominations appointed a Joint Listening Committee for Homosexuality Concerns with three tasks in mind.

> 1. To care for gay-lesbian persons and their families in the General Conference and Mennonite Church by listening to their alienation and pain in the church and society.
> 2. To encourage/facilitate dialogue between persons of various perspectives concerning homosexuality, and to foster continuing theological discernment in the church on this issue.
> 3. To make recommendations to the Mennonite Board of Congregational Ministry (MC) and the Commission on Education (GCMC) regarding policy, program, and church life in order to deal with alienation and hurt.

The Listening Committee has experienced some frustration in its work. At Bethlehem '83, the joint MC-GCMC Conference, booth space was granted to BMC but subsequently denied under pressures from conservative delegates. Instead, the Seminar Committee approved a workshop on recovery programs for homosexuals. Protests from BMC against this alleged homophobic injustice resulted in giving them their own workshop.

At the 1990 Mennonite World Conference in Winnipeg, the work of the Listening Committee was further frustrated from the other side when the BMC workshop was structured in advance to rule out certain kinds of questions typically asked by conservative Mennonites and BICs. It remains to be seen whether the Listening Committee can help the members of BMC and our conference commissions and congregations to move from fear and rejection to mutual respect and a more trusting dialogue.

Factors in the Discernment of this Issue

The Incidence of Homosexuality. One problem in achieving better dialogue is the lack of reliable information about the whole subject of homosexuality, beginning with the question of its incidence or frequency of occurrence. BMC leaders often begin their workshops with the claim that 10% of the population has a homosexual orientation. The 10% statistic is supposed to come from the Kinsey reports of 1948 (males) and 1953 (females)—widely recognized as the most systematic and comprehensive survey of the sexual behavior of men and women in America to date. Actually the Kinsey reports defined homosexuality as a continuum along a scale from fully heterosexual to fully homosexual with five intermediate points, measured by psychic responses (erotic arousal, fantasies, etc.) as well as overt experience and behavior:

1. Predominantly heterosexual, with incidental homosexual experience.
2. Basically heterosexual, with significant homosexual experience.
3. Bisexual, with significant heterosexual and homosexual experience.
4. Basically homosexual, with significant heterosexual experience.
5. Predominantly homosexual, with incidental heterosexual experience.
   (Kinsey, 638)

According to the Kinsey reports, only about 4% of all males and 2-3% of all females are exclusively homosexual throughout their lives. However, 10% of the males and about half that proportion of the females were basically or predominantly homosexual for at least three years of their adult lives.

As part of the CMP II Research Project, we tried to gauge the incidence of homosexuality among Mennonites and BICs by asking two questions.

1. What is your sexual orientation?
   a. Heterosexual
   b. Bisexual
   c. Homosexual

2. Have you engaged in homosexual acts?
   a. Frequently
   b. Occasionally
   c. Once or a few times
   d. Never

Only seven out of 3,087 respondents declared themselves as homosexually oriented (two-thirds of 1%). Eighty-two respondents identified themselves as bisexual (48 males, 40 females). These statistics are probably unreliable, given that 415 persons in our sample failed to respond to this question—some perhaps for lack of understanding of what the terms meant and others for fear of identifying themselves as homosexual or bisexual, even on an anonymous questionnaire.

There may have been less confusion and secrecy in responding to the second question, to which only 38 persons failed to reply. Nevertheless, no one replied "frequently," only 11 (four-tenths of 1%) replied "occasionally," 46 (1.5%) replied "once or a few times," and 2,992 (97%) replied "never."

In the U.S., by comparison (according to the 1991 Patterson-Kim survey, 137), 14% of the general population has at some time engaged in sex with someone of the same sex. If we assumed that our CMP figures were accurate, we would have to conclude that the incidence of homosexual orientation and behavior among Mennonites and BICs is negligible and certainly not comparable to the Kinsey and the Patterson/Kim reports of American men and women.

If our statistics are unreliable, we would have to surmise that the high degree of rejection in our churches has already forced most homosexually oriented and/or practicing members to depart, and that many of those remaining feel compelled to deny their homosexuality.

The Rejection of Gay and Lesbian Persons. We discovered that 77% of our respondents as a whole would not accept practicing homosexual persons as members of their congregations. Even if they were homosexually oriented but not practicing, 29% would still not accept them as members. Separatist-type churches are by far the least accepting, with a 90% rejection of practicing and a 37% rejection of non-practicing homosexuals as members. Liberal-type churches were the most accepting, but even here the rejection rate was 70% for practicing and 21% for non-practicing homosexuals.

We found that not only do the vast majority of Mennonite and BIC respondents (92%) condemn homosexual acts as always wrong, but also that the percentage increased by six points since 1972, following the ratification of the 1986/1987 MC/GCMC resolutions on this issue. This further complicates the process of continuing to work toward better communication with the gay and lesbian Christians in our midst, because many members believe the matter was settled and these people must now be disciplined accordingly.

The Nature of Homosexuality. This factor in the discussion pivots on the question, "Is homosexuality a natural or unnatural condition?" The five most quoted biblical passages on the subject emphasize the "unnaturalness" of the condition.

> 1. Gen. 19:1-29: A case of intended homosexual gang rape in Sodom.
> 2. Lev. 18:22; 20:13: Male homosexuality condemned as an abomination punishable by death.
> 3. 1 Cor. 6:9; 1 Tim. 1:10: Presupposes and reaffirms the Mosaic condemnation with particular reference to the sin of pederasty, i.e., anal inter course with boys.
> 4. Rom. 1:18-32: Condemns both male and female homosexuality as substitution of unnatural for natural genital intercourse—a particularly reprehensible result of the willful human distortion of God's creation. (Hayes, 18-19)

Gay and lesbian Christians insist that none of these texts applies to a wholesome consensual relationship within a permanent covenant of love. They are condemnations of promiscuous acts of heterosexual persons who "exchanged natural intercourse for unnatural" (Rom. 1:16b) and not applicable to Christians who are "naturally" of homosexual orientation.

A redemptive, healing watershed is claimed to have been reached in the agonizing faith journeys of gay and lesbian Christians when they finally accept the givenness (yes, giftedness) of the way they were allegedly created. These people claim that their homosexuality is not something they chose but something they discovered about themselves.

> We have learned that our lesbian and gay identities are gifts of God to be cherished and honored, and sin is whatever we and others do to hide and denigrate this gift. . . . I realize that for many sincere and faithful Christians, these claims may cause a near visceral reaction as they fly in the face of many long-held beliefs. I know that, for it is with those beliefs that I, too, began. It has been a long and at times difficult faith journey to move from fear and self-loathing to accepting and embracing God's gift of my homosexuality. Yet, quite simply, I had no choice. God kept nudging me on. It was trust in God that gave me the courage to rethink the issues in an environment so very hostile to my very being. Yet it is into this faith journey of new reflection that we who are gay and Christian invite the larger Christian communi-

ty to listen to and discern the movements of the Spirit in our lives. (Spencer, 22-23)

The Causes of Homosexuality. There are theological theories of causation and scientific theories, but no convincing breakthroughs to date. As reviewed above, biblicists argue that the root-cause is human sin—not just the sinfulness of any one or two persons but the twistedness of the entire environment in which we live, the consequences of centuries of rebellion against our Creator. The opposite point of view is that heterosexuality and homosexuality are both givens in God's creation.

Scientific theories are no less far-ranging. In past decades they have tended to polarize around biological and environmental influences, but "there is now a substantial body of evidence to suggest that human beings are born with a sexual potential and that heterosexual, homosexual, bisexual, or asexual preferences unfold during the experiences of childhood and adolescence" (Sexuality, 247).

There are *genetic theories* that homosexuality can be hereditary. There are hormonal theories that sex hormones, particularly the hormone androgen, influence the fetus in the direction of masculinity or femininity.

There are *psychoanalytic theories* that "either boys are too fearful of wanting their mothers sexually and thus turn from her and all like her to the safety of those with penises, or they experience intense relations with the mother and so identify with her femaleness that they take the same love objects (males)" (HSB, 248). This theory is applied to female homosexuality with reverse gender.

There are *learning theories* which put more emphasis on environmental conditioning of sexual preferences, such as home environments in which the child experiences difficulty identifying with the same-sex parent.

The newest theory was published in August, 1991, in the journal *Science.* A behavioral neuroscientist at the National Institute of Mental Health allegedly discovered that the brains of homosexual men are structurally different from those of heterosexual men in a region of the brain thought to influence sexual orientation. His working hypothesis is that homosexuality is caused by this variation in brain structure.

Scientific researchers will continue to probe for causes of homosexuality. Meanwhile we would be well advised in our ongoing discernment process to admit that we do not know enough to make moral judgments that arbitrarily reject persons of another sexual orientation and thereby rule them out of the kingdom of Christ.

Toward Further Discernment of Issues Like This

How then are we to continue to work at issues like this? In his book, *Trackless Wastes and Stars to Steer By,* Michael A. King, book editor for Herald Press, offers one possibility. With concepts borrowed from MB missiologist Paul Hiebert, King describes how three different models of the church affect moral discernment in the congregation. The *bounded model* is a separatist church that specifies clearly who is in and who is out.

> You know apples don't belong in the category *oranges.* You can also know whether George and Jane belong in the category *Christian* or *church.* You know that George, who gives intellectual assent to his church's doctrine, and agrees to live his life by its rules, is in. You know that Jane, who admits to doubts about certain doctrinal statements and drinks forbidden wine, is out. (King, 116)

The *unbounded model* is an integrationist church in which there are few boundaries. It is a "fuzzy set" kind of church in which

> you could, perhaps, be a quarter Buddhist, an eighth Shinto, a ninth Hindu, and the rest maybe secular humanist. This kind of fuzziness is common, for instance, in Japan. Fundamentalist George can be in if he wants (though he probably doesn't). So can Jane, whether she drinks wine or not. (King, 118)

The *centered model* focuses on the center—Jesus Christ—rather than on the boundaries. As Hiebert wrote,

> it is created by defining a center, and the relationship of things to that center. Some things may be far from the center, but they are related to or moving *toward* the center; therefore they are part of the centered set. On the other hand, some objects may be near the center but are moving *away* from it so they are not a part of the set. The set is made up of all things related to or moving towards the center. (Hiebert, 423)

If candidates for membership are willing to be directed to the center, they are accepted, even though still distant from the center. On the other hand, if the basic concerns of long-standing members are not directed toward the center, they might sound pious like the Pharisees of old—but really be moving away from Jesus.

The *bounded model* discerns moral issues in clear rights and wrongs. To maintain moral purity it emphasizes separation from the world, separation defined both geographically and moralistically. Since the official MC/GCMC position on homosexual practice is that it is wrong, even when a same-sex couple are confining their relationship within a Christian covenant, the couple is barred from church membership.

Because of the complexities of living in a pluralistic society, the *unbounded model* avoids making any judgment about the rightness and wrongness of an individual's behavior. Unbounded groups prefer to give people the freedom to make those decisions for themselves.

The *centered model*, which is no less complex in its principle and process of discernment—to seek the mind of Christ and to act accordingly—has implications of its own for moral decision making. Not everyone is accepted into membership, but only those who earnestly want to follow Christ. Membership entails affirmation that Christ's truth is always greater than ours and that our ways are often not his ways. This is true even though Christ has given us the mandate to make binding and loosing decisions to the extent we have discerned his mind on a given issue.

In their tendency to polarize on moral issues like this, congregations (not to mention members within a given congregation) are inclined toward either bounded or unbounded models. Evidence for this conclusion comes from a tabulation of fifty-one letters to the editor of *The Mennonite*, the semi-monthly magazine of the GCMC. In the February 12, 1991 issue, the editors featured a pro and con discussion of the controversial issue of homosexuality. Responses of readers were emotional and often laced with anger and venom. Using King's definitions, the writer tabulated the responses by the method of content analysis as follows:

1. Reflecting the bounded model: 23 responses, 45%
2. Reflecting the unbounded model: 16 responses, 31%
3. Reflecting the centered model: 7 responses, 14%
4. Unclear: 5 responses, 10%

Seventy-six percent of the responses were polarized between bounded and unbounded attitudes, typified by the following selected excerpts, followed by one representing the centered model:

Bounded Attitude

I am appalled at the Feb. 12th issue. I did not believe this kind of teaching was possible in our traditional Ananabaptist-Mennonite churches. The lead article reminds me of the false teachers in the epistle of Jude and the church of Pergamum in Revelation 2:14-15. If this is the way our General Conference Mennonite Church leadership interprets the Bible, we are in for a rude awakening, a mass exodus of individuals, churches, and

Unbounded Attitude

Hooray for reopening the discussion of homosexuality. Thanks to the honest writers and to the magazine for compiling such a representative group of articles. This type of action dispels some of the incongruities that I have felt as I have grown up with a dual outlook: having a gay father and attending a Mennonite church. . . . Many of these homosexual people are in our churches and are actively searching to determine God's perhaps district conferences. . . . My two sons-in-law had high regard for the Mennonite church until the perverted teaching of homosexuality was published. I am a great proponent of dialogue in our papers. I have nothing against homosexuals or their relatives who are caught between their homosexual children and the church. One author rationalizes that homosexual orientation is not a sin because the individual was born that way and did not choose to be homosexual. None of us chose to be sinful when we were born with Adam's sinful nature (Romans 5:12).

People could be born with homosexual orientation. *I object, however, to the practice and the acceptance of such people into the church.* A homosexual must come under the atoning blood of Christ and "go and sin no more" (John 5:14, 8:11).

will for the church. But recently I have also seen churches begin to search outside their traditional beliefs and fears as they allow homosexual people and/or family members to share their experiences and suffering. The church needs to open itself for this to happen.

The articles were intelligent and articulate and provided the best analysis of Scriptures relating to the subject that I have read. All messages from God are filtered through our human minds; they are unavoidably colored by our interpretation and understanding, no matter how divinely inspired. . . .

I think it is shameful for Mennonites to deny or place conditions on membership and participation in our churches based on a person's sexual orientation. Who is any of us to judge a person's relationship with God?

Centered Attitude

We are quick to express our opposition to killing in a war, but our churches, to a great extent, either ignore or even condone the hurt they inflict on homosexuals. Regardless of what we may think about homosexuality, such shoddy treatment is not worthy of Christians who pride themselves in helping the needy.

As a deacon I have had occasion to "examine" prospective church members. *My interest was in their faith in God and Christ, their ideas about spiritual growth and what they felt they wanted to get and give from affiliation with a church.* None of this suggested questions of heterosexuality or homosexuality, marriage or non-marriage, educated or not educated, curled or straight hair, color of skin. The criteria for assessing an individual's Christianity (suitable for church membership) does not include such questions. A homosexual individual can have a saving faith in Jesus Christ the same as a hetero-sexual individual.

The last excerpt represents the *centered model* of the church but does not specify how "faith in God and Christ" leads to reconciliation and redemption. Michael King would put an issue like this at the church's center rather than at its boundaries. If we start with the MC/GCMC statements on homosexuality, we would declare at the center that we believe homosexual behavior to be wrong. Yet we would not immediately conclude that therefore gay persons have no place in the membership of the church, which would be out of keeping with the concern of Christ for rejected people. King would say to the homosexual, "This is our stance. We're willing, however, to process this issue with you as one of us, as one who stands within the circle of this family of God" (King, 133-4).

Summary and Conclusion

In this chapter we explored the congregational discernment theme in relation to three moral issues—abortion, capital punishment, and homosexuality. Abortion is an issue on which Americans are split down the middle, while Mennonites and BICs are mostly opposed, except in cases of endangerment of the woman's life, rape, and serious defect in the embryo. Capital punishment is an issue in which Mennonites and BICs are ambivalent while Americans are mostly in favor of the death penalty.

Discernment of the homosexuality issue is fraught with more tension among Mennonites than the other two issues. The MCs and GCs thought they came to closure on the subject in nearly identical resolutions. However, due to the protestations of gay and lesbian persons in their midst, the issue has not gone away and perhaps should not according to the "Confession" and "Covenant" parts of the resolutions.

What we need is a better way to work at not only this issue but others like premarital and extramarital intercourse, divorce and remarriage, cheating on income tax returns, payment of war taxes, use of beverage alcohol, etc. The King/Hiebert concept of the centered model of the church provides the key to a third way—acceptance of a wider degree of moral pluralism at the boundaries of the church, on one hand, and the intentional exercise of a Christ-centered authority to bind and loose on the other.

Certainly a book like *The Day America Told the Truth* could be a new impetus for us to reflect anew on where our people are in relation to the moral degeneracy of our time. The issues we would then need to discern are not only the three dealt with in this chapter but also the more taken-for-granted realities of the sexual satiation of our culture affecting heterosexuals and homosexuals alike. Also requiring attention would be the increasing crime rates resulting from the failures of many of us to be absolutely honest and law-abiding in our own lifestyle and all the other moral compromises we make when we seek first the kingdom of mammon rather than the kingdom of Christ.

Discussion Questions

1. What, if any, are the special perspectives that Mennonites and Brethren in Christ bring to the discernment of the abortion issue?

2. Do you agree that what is lawful may not be morally right? Can a Christian believe both that our laws should not prohibit abortion and that it is often or always morally wrong to have one?

3. What can a congregation do when a member family is facing the pregnancy of a teenage daughter or the involvement of a teenage son?

4. Are the arguments for capital punishment sufficient to justify the desire for vengeance in our society? To justify executing some innocent people? To justify the degrading moral effect that it has on society? To justify executing many more members of impoverished minority groups than wealthy and influential persons?

5. What do you think of the assumption that some people are homosexual in orientation but not in behavior? That Jesus would not reject homosexually-oriented persons the way we often do? That a person can be homosexually oriented and still be a faithful Christian? That some gay Christians might think of their homosexuality as a gift of God?

6. Do you agree that a centered model of discernment is preferable to bounded or unbounded models? Would a centered model be too permissive and lead to neglect of member accountability?

References

Ainley, Stephen C.
"Communal Commitment and Individualism," *Anabaptist-Mennonite Identities in Ferment*. Elkhart, Ind.: Institute of Mennonite Studies, 1990.

Alderfer, Edwin and Helen
"What We Are Learning," *Life and Values*, Edwin and Helen Alderfer, eds. Scottdale: Mennonite Publishing House, 1974.

Barrett, Lois
"Flowing Like a River," *Why I Am a Mennonite: Essays on Mennonite Identity*, Harry Loewen, ed. Kitchener, Ont.: Herald Press, 1988.

BC
Proceedings of the Study Conference on the Believers' Church, P. K. Regier, ed. North Newton, Kan.: Mennonite Press, 1955.

Bellah, Robert N., et al.
Habits of the Heart: Individualism and Commitment in American Life. Berkeley: Univ. of Calif. Press, 1985.

Bender, Harold S.
A. "Outside Influences on Mennonite Thought," *Mennonite Life*, II, January 1955.
B. "Ministry," *The Mennonite Encyclopedia*, III. Scottdale: Herald Press, 1957.

Bender, Ross T.
The People of God: A Mennonite Interpretation of the Free Church Tradition. Scottdale: Herald Press, 1971.

Bennett, John C.
Christian Ethics and Social Policy. New York: Scribners and Sons, 1946.

Benson, Peter L., and Carolyn H. Eklin
Effective Christian Education: A National Study of Protestant Congregations. Minneapolis: Search Institute, 1990.

Berger, Peter L.
A. *The Precarious Vision: A Sociologist Looks at Social Fictions and Christian Faith.*
    Garden City, N.Y.: Doubleday and Co., 1961.
B. *The Noise of Solemn Assemblies: Christian Commitment and the Religious Estab-*
    lishment in America. Garden City. N.Y.: Doubleday and Co., 1961.

Bettenson, Henry
    Documents of the Christian Church. New York: Oxford Univ. Press, 1947.

BI
    "Biblical Interpretation in the Life of the Church," *Proceedings [of the] Menno-*
    nite Church, General Assembly, Estes Park, Colorado. June 18-24, 1977.

BIC
    Minutes of General Conference of Brethren in Christ from 1871 to 1904. Harrison-
    burg, Va., 1904.

Bower, William C.
    Christ and Christian Education. New York: Abingdon-Cokesbury Press, 1943.

Bowman, John W.
    The Intention of Jesus. Philadelphia: Westminster Press, 1943.

Brandt, Herbert
    "Pastoral Letter: A Stronger Bond of Unity," *The Christian Leader,* January 16,
    1990.

Brown, Dale W.
    Biblical Pacifism: A Peace Church Perspective. Elgin, Ill: Brethren Press, 1986.

Brown, Robert McAfee
    "Two Books by Berger: An Assembly of Solemn Noises," *Union Seminary*
    Quarterly Review, 17:4, May 1962.

Brunk II, George
    "The MC/GC Merger," *Sword and Trumpet* (January 1992).

Brunk III, George
A. "The Exclusiveness of Jesus Christ," *Jesus Christ and the Mission of the Church.*
    Elkhart, Ind., and Newton, Kan.: Mennonite Church and General Confer-
    ence Mennonite Church, 1989.
B. "MCs and GCs: Some Comparisons," *Gospel Herald,* 81:49 (Nov. 29, 1988).

Burkholder, J. Lawrence
A. "Social Implications of Mennonite Doctrines," *Proceedings of the Twelfth Con-*
    ference on Mennonite Educational and Cultural Problems. Elkhart, Ind.: Menno-
    nite Biblical Seminary, 1959.
B. "The Peace Churches as Communities of Discernment," *The Christian*
    Century, 80:36, September 4, 1963.
C. "Theological Education for the Believers' Church," *Concern* No. 17, Febru-
    ary 1969.

Burkholder, J. Richard
"Peace," *The Mennonite Encyclopedia*, V. Scottdale: Herald Press, 1990.

Bushnell, Horace
Christian Nurture. New Haven, Conn.: Yale Univ. Press, 1947.

Clark, Stephen B.
Man and Woman in Christ: An Examination of the Roles of Men and Women in the Light of Scripture and the Social Sciences. Ann Arbor, Mich.: Servant Books, 1980.

Correll, Ernst
"The Congressional Debates on the Mennonite Immigration from Russia, 1873-74," *Mennonite Quarterly Review*, 20:3, July 1946.

Cosby, Gordon
"Not Renewal, But Reformation," *Renewal*, 3:3, April 1963.

Dodd, C. H.
History and the Gospel. New York: Scribner's Sons, 1938.

Downey, G.
"Syrian Antioch," *The Interpreter's Dictionary of the Bible*, I. New York: Abingdon Press, 1962.

Dueck, Al
"Who Are My People?" *The Perils of Professionalism*, Phyllis Pellman Good and Donald B. Kraybill, eds. Scottdale: Herald Press, 1982.

Durkheim, Emile
The Elementary Forms of Religious Life. New York: Collier Books, 1961.

Ediger, Elmer
"A Christian's Political Responsibility," *Mennonite Life*, July 1956.

Ediger, Peter J.
Lemon Drops and Other Childhood Memories. Las Vegas, Nev.: Published by the author, 1991.

Epstein, I.
"Halachah," *The Interpreter's Dictionary of the Bible*, I. New York: Abingdon Press, 1962.

ESA
"Can My Vote Be Biblical?" Washington, D.C.: *Evangelicals for Social Action*, n.d.

Fretz, J. Winfield
"Should Mennonites Participate in Politics?" *Mennonite Life*, 11:3, July 1956.

Friedmann, Robert
"The Doctrine of the Two Worlds," *The Recovery of the Anabaptist Vision*, Guy F. Hershberger, ed. Scottdale: Herald Press, 1957.

Friesen, Duane K.
"Biblical Authority: The Contemporary Theological Debate," *Mennonite Life*, 44:3, September 1989.

Garber, Julie
"Promoting Peace in Baghdad," *The Church of the Brethren Messenger*, March 1991.

Gingerich, Melvin
A. *Service for Peace*. Akron, Pa.: The Mennonite Central Committee, 1949.
B. "Historic Peace Churches," *Mennonite Encyclopedia*, IV. Scottdale: Herald Press, 1959.

Green, Michael
Evangelism in the Early Church. Grand Rapids, Mich.: Wm. B. Eerdmans Publishing Co., 1970.

Greer, Scott
Social Organization. New York: Random House, 1955.

Harder, Helmut
A. *Accountability in the Church: A Study Guide for Congregations*. Winnipeg, Man.: Conference of Mennonites in Canada, 1985.
B. *Witnessing to Christ in Today's World*. Nappanee, Ind.: Evangel Press; Newton, Kan.: Faith and Life Press; Scottdale: Mennonite Publishing House, 1989.

Harder, Leland
A. "The Russian Mennonites and American Democracy Under Grant," *From the Steppes to the Prairies*, Cornelius Krahn, ed. Newton, Kan.: Mennonite Publication Office, 1949.
B. "Church Planting: Always a Mystery," *The Mennonite*, 98:8, April 12, 1983.
C. *The Sources of Swiss Anabaptism*. Scottdale: Herald Press, 1985.
D. "Mennonite Denominational Patterns of Faith and Life," *AMBS Bulletin*, 53:3 (May 1990).
E. *Fact Book of Congregational Membership*. Newton, Kan.: Faith and Life Press, 1990.
F. "The Concept of Discipleship in Christian Education," *Religious Education*, 63:4, July 1963.
G. "Changing Forms of the Church and Her Witness," *Concern*, No. 12, February 1966, pp. 3-31.

Hayes, Richard B.
"Awaiting the Redemption of Our Bodies," *Sojourners*, 20:6, July 1991.

Hays, William L.
Statistics for the Social Sciences. New York: Holt, Rinehart and Winston, 1973.

Henderson, Robert F.
Joy to the World: An Introduction to Kingdom Evangelism. Atlanta: John Knox Press, 1980

Hershberger, Guy F.
A. *War, Peace, and Nonresistance*. Scottdale: Herald Press, 1946.
B. "Pacifism," *Mennonite Encyclopedia*, IV. Scottdale: Herald Press, 1959.

Hiebert, Paul
"The Category 'Christian' in the Mission Task," *International Review of Missions*, 272, July 1983.

Hostetler, Beulah
"Mennonite Church," *The Mennonite Encyclopedia*, V. Scottdale: Herald Press, 1990.

Howard, Wilbert F.
"The First Paraclete Saying," *The Interpreter's Bible*, VIII. New York: Abingdon-Cokesbury Press, 1952.

HSB
"Human Sexual Behavior," *The New Encyclopedia Brittanica*, 27, Macropaedia. Chicago: Encyclopedia Brittanica, Inc., 1982.

HS
Human Sexuality in the Christian Life. Newton, Kan.: Faith and Life Press; Scottdale: Mennonite Publishing House, 1985.

IEC
MC/GC Integration Committee, "Integration or Cooperation?" *Gospel Herald*, 84:42 (Oct. 22, 1991.

Janzen, Peter
Memoirs of Peter Janzen. Published by the author, 1921.

Jewett, Paul K.
Man as Male and Female: A Study in Sexual Relationships from a Theological Point of View. Grand Rapids, Mich.: Eerdmans, 1974.

Johnson, Luke T.
Decision Making in the Church: A Biblical Model. Philadelphia: Fortress Press, 1983.

Juhnke, James C.
A. "Political Attitudes," *Mennonite Encyclopedia*, V. Scottdale: Herald Press, 1990.
B. *A People of Two Kingdoms: The Political Acculturation of Kansas Mennonites*. Newton, Kan.: Faith and Life Press, 1975.

C. *Vision, Doctrine, War: Mennonite Identity and Organization in America.* Scott-dale: Herald Press, 1989.

Kauffman, J. Howard, and Leo Driedger
The Mennonite Mosaic: Identity and Modernization. Scottdale: Herald Press, 1991.

Kauffman, J. Howard, and Leland Harder
Anabaptists Four Centuries Later: A Profile of Five Mennonite and Brethren in Christ Denominations. Scottdale: Herald Press, 1975.

Kaufman, Donald D.
"Taxes," *Mennonite Encyclopedia*, V. Scottdale: Herald Press, 1990.

Kaufman, Gordon D.
A. "Should Mennonites Register for the Draft?" *The Mennonite*, June 8, 1948.
B. "Nonresistance and Responsibility," *Concern*, No. 6, November 1958.

Keeney, William
"Peace Activism," *Mennonite Encyclopedia*, V. Scottdale: Herald Press, 1990.

King, Michael A.
Trackless Wastes and Stars to Steer By: Christian Identity in a Homeless Age. Scott-dale: Herald Press, 1990.

Kinsey, Alfred, et al.
Sexual Behavior in the Human Male. Philadelphia: W. B. Saunders Co., 1948.

Klaassen, Walter
A. "New Presbyter Is Old Priest Writ Large," *Concern*, No. 17, February 1969.
B. "Anabaptism," *Mennonite Encyclopedia*, V. Scottdale: Herald Press, 1990.
C. "Fig Leaves and Anabaptists," *Why I Am a Mennonite: Essays on Mennonite Identity*, Harry Loewen, ed. Kitchener, Ont.: Herald Press, 1988.
D. "The Quest for Anabaptist Identity," *Anabaptist-Mennonite Identities in Ferment*, Leo Driedger and Leland Harder, eds. Elkhart, Ind.: Institute for Mennonite Studies, 1990.

Koontz, Ted
A. "Church-State Relations," *Mennonite Encyclopedia*, V. Scottdale: Herald Press, 1990.
B. "Mennonites and 'Postmodernity,' " *The Mennonite Quarterly Review*, 63:4, October 1989.

Kraemer, Hendrik
A Theology of the Laity. Philadelphia: Westminster Press, 1958.

Krahn, Cornelius
"Ministry," *Mennonite Encyclopedia*, III. Scottdale: Herald Press, 1957.

Kraus, C. Norman
"Shifting Mennonite Theological Orientations," *Anabaptist-Mennonite Identities in Ferment*, Leo Driedger and Leland Harder, eds. Elkhart, Ind.: Institute of Mennonite Studies, 1990.

Kraybill, Donald B.
A. *The Upside-Down Kingdom*. Scottdale: Herald Press, 1978.
B. "Modernity and Modernization," *Anabaptist-Mennonite Identities in Ferment*, Leo Driedger and Leland Harder, eds. Elkhart, Ind.: Institute of Mennonite Studies, 1990.
C. "Civil Religion, United States," *Mennonite Encyclopedia*, V. Scottdale: Herald Press, 1990.

Kraybill, Paul
"Inter-Mennonite Cooperation," *The Mennonite Encyclopedia*, V. Scottdale: Herald Press, 1990.

Leatherman, Daniel
The Political Socialization of Students in the Mennonite Secondary Schools. M.A. dissertation, Univ. of Chicago, 1960.

Lewis, C. S.
The Screwtape Letters. New York: The Macmillan Co., 1948.

Loewen, Harry, ed.
Why I Am a Mennonite. Kitchener, Ont.: Herald Press, 1988.

Loewen, Howard
One Lord, One Church, One Hope, and One God: Mennonite Confessions of Faith. Elkhart, Ind.: Institute of Mennonite Studies, 1985.

Martens, Hedy L.
"Mennonite Identity in Creative Tension," *Why I Am a Mennonite*, Harry Loewen, ed. Kitchener, Ont.: Herald Press, 1988.

Martin, Ernest D.
The Story and Witness of the Christian Way. Scottdale: Mennonite Publishing House, 1971.

Marty, Martin
The Pro and Con Books of Religious America. Waco, Tex.: Word Books, 1975.

MBC
A. *Yearbook of the 50th Session of the General Conference of the Mennonite Brethren Church*. Hillsboro, Kan.: M.B. Publishing House, 1966.
B. *Yearbook of the 54th Session of the General Conference of the Mennonite Brethren Church*. Hillsboro, Kan.: M.B. Publishing House, 1978.

McPhee, Arthur G.
Friendship Evangelism: The Caring Way to Share Your Faith. Harrisonburg, Va.: Choice Books, 1978.

MCF
"The Mennonite Confession of Faith," *The Story and Witness of the Christian Way*, Ernest D. Martin, ed. Scottdale: Mennonite Publishing House, 1971.

ME
The Mennonite Encyclopedia, I, II, III, IV, V. Scottdale: Herald Press, 1955, 1956, 1957, 1959, 1990.

Mead, Frank S.
Handbook of Denominations in the United States. Nashville: Abingdom Press, 1970.

Miller, John A.
The Christian Way: A Guide to the Christian Life Based on the Sermon on the Mount. Scottdale: Herald Press, 1969.

Miller, Paul M.
Servant of God's Servants. Scottdale: Herald Press, 1964.

Moore, John A.
Anabaptist Portraits. Scottdale, Herald Press, 1982.

Nafziger, Estel W.
"The Mennonite Ethic in the Weberian Framework," *Explorations in Entrepreneurial History*, 2:1, Summer 1965.

Neufeld, John
A. "An Experiment in Preaching," *The Mennonite*, 95:43, Nov. 25, 1980.
B. "Paul's Teaching on the Status of Men and Women," *Study Guide on Women*, ed. Herta Funk. Newton, Kan.: Faith and Life Press, 1984.

Nussbaum, Stan
"Evangelical Mennonite Church, United States," *The Mennonite Encyclopedia*, V. Scottdale: Herald Press, 1990.

Oyer, John S.
"Ethics, Aesthetics, and Mennonites," *Why I Am a Mennonite: Essays on Mennonite Identity*, Harry Loewen, ed. Kitchener, Ont.: Herald Press, 1988.

Pannabecker, S. F.
Open Doors: The History of the General Conference Mennonite Church. Newton, Kan.: Faith and Life Press, 1971.

Patterson, James, and Peter Kim
The Day America Told the Truth. New York: Prentice Hall Press, 1991.

Peachey, J. Lorne
"Pastorate Project Meeting Looks for Elusive Solutions; Pastor-Church Relations Problems Easier to Identify than Solve," *Mennonite Weekly Review*, 69:52, Dec. 26, 1991.

Poettcker, Henry
"General Conference Mennonite Church," *The Mennonite Encyclopedia*, V. Scottdale: Herald Press, 1990.

Ramseyer, Robert
"Let's Cooperate, Not Merge," *The Mennonite*, 103:16, Aug. 23, 1988.

Recommendation
"Recommendation on Exploring MC/GC Integration," *The Mennonite*, 106:20, Oct. 22, 1991.

Redekop, John H.
A. *Making Political Decisions: A Christian Perspective*. Scottdale: Herald Press, 1972.
B. "Involvement in the Political Order," *Christian Leader*, Sept. 27, 1977.
C. "Mennonites and Politics in Canada and the United States," *Journal of Mennonite Studies*, 1, 1983.
D. "Mennonite Political Conservatism: Paradox or Contradiction," *Mennonite Images: Historical, Cultural, and Literary Essays Dealing with Mennonite Issues*, Harry Loewen, ed. Winnipeg, Man.: Hyperion Press, 1980.
E. "More than Ethnic: Redefining Mennonite Identity," *Why I Am a Mennonite: Essays on Mennonite Identity*. Kitchener, Ont.: Herald Press, 1988.
F. *A People Apart: Ethnicity and the Mennonite Brethren*. Winnipeg, Man.: Kindred Press, 1987.

Regier, Austin
"The Faith of a Convict," *The Christian Century*, Feb. 2, 1949.

Roehrlkepartain, Eugene C.
"What Makes Faith Mature?" *The Christian Century*, May 9, 1990.

Rose, Stephen
"Whence the Rugged Individualist?" *Renewal*, 3:9, December 1963.

Sawatsky, Rodney J.
"The One and the Many: The Recovery of Mennonite Pluralism," *Anabaptism Revisited*, Walter Klaassen, ed. Scottdale: Herald Press, 1991.

Scanzoni, Letha, and Nancy Hardesty
All We're Meant to Be: A Biblical Approach to Women's Liberation. Waco, Tex.: Word Books, 1974.

Schuller, Lyle, ed.
The Parish Paper, a monthly publication of The Yokefellow Institute, 920 Earlham Dr., Richmond, IN 47374, 1972-present.

Schlabach, Theron F.
"Choosing the Strengths and Minimizing the Weaknesses," *Gospel Herald*, 84:42 (Oct. 22, 1991).

Schoedel, William R.
   Ignatius of Antioch: A Commentary on the Letters of Ignatius of Antioch. Philadelphia: Fortress Press, 1985.

Sexuality
   "Sex and Sexuality," *The New Encyclopedia Brittanica*, 27, Macropaedia. Chicago: Encyclopedia Brittanica, Inc., 1990.

Sherrill, Lewis J.
   The Rise of Christian Education. New York: Macmillan Co., 1950.

Sider, E. Morris
   "Brethren in Christ Churches, General Conference," *The Mennonite Encyclopedia*, V. Scottdale: Herald Press, 1990.

Sider, Ronald J.
   "God's People Reconciling," *Proceedings of the Mennonite World Conference, XI Assembly, Strasbourg.* Lombard, Ill.: Mennonite World Conference, 1984.

Siemens, Mark
   "Waging Peace: What Four Mennonite Churches Are Doing," *The Christian Leader*, Oct. 18, 1983.

Smith, C. Henry
   The Story of the Mennonites, 3rd edition. Newton, Kan.: Mennonite Publication Office, 1957.

Smucker, Donovan E.
   "A Mennonite Critique of the Pacifist Movement," *Mennonite Quarterly Review*, 20:1, January 1946.

Smucker, Joseph
   "Religious Community and Individualism: Conceptual Adaptations by One Group of Mennonites," *Journal for the Scientific Study of Religion*, 25.

Spencer, Dan
   "The Risks of Reconciliation," *Sojourners*, 20:6, July 1991.

Steiner, Jan
   "The Church Did Not Meet My Needs," *The Mennonite*, 83:6, Feb. 6, 1968.

Stoltzfus, Gene
   "A Call to Peacemaking," *Mennonite World Handbook: Mennonites in Global Witness.* Carol Stream, Ill.: Mennonite World Conference, 1990.

Stoltzfus, Grant
   "A People Apart and a People Involved—the 'Old Mennonites,' " *Christian Living*, 17:6, June 1970.

Swartley, Willard M.
Slavery, Sabbath, War, and Women: Case Issues in Biblical Interpretation. Scottdale: Herald Press, 1983.

Toews, John B., Abram G. Konrad, and Alvin Dueck
Direction, 14:2, Fall 1985.

Toews, John E.
Jesus Christ, the Convener of the Church. Elkhart, Ind., and Newton, Kan., Mennonite Church and General Conference Mennonite Church, 1989.

Toews, Paul
"Fundamentalism," *Mennonite Encyclopedia,* V. Scottdale: Herald Press, 1990.

Unger, Walter
"Mennonite: A Way of Following Christ," *Why I Am a Mennonite: Essays on Mennonite Identity,* Harry Loewen, ed. Kitchener, Ont.: Herald Press, 1988.

Walters, Leroy
"Abortion," *Life and Values,* Edwin and Helen Alderfer, eds. Scottdale: Mennonite Publishing House, 1974.

Wenger, J. C.
History of the Mennonites of the Franconia Conference. Scottdale: Mennonite Publishing House, 1938.

Westerhoff III, John H.
Will Our Children Have Faith? New York: Seabury Press, 1976.

Wiebe, Katie Funk
"Can the Church Survive the Professionalization of Its Leadership?" *The Mennonite,* 105:6, March 27, 1990.

Wiebe, Rudy
Peace Shall Destroy Many. Toronto: McClelland and Stewart Ltd., 1962.

Wink, Walter
A. *The Bible in Human Transformation: A New Paradigm for Biblical Study.* Philadelphia: Fortress Press, 1973.
B. *Transforming Bible Study.* New York: Abingdon Press, 1990.

Winter, Gibson
The New Creation as Metropolis. New York: The Macmillan Co., 1963.

WML
Works of Martin Luther. Philadelphia, 1915

Yinger, J. Milton
The Scientific Study of Religion. New York: Macmillan Publishing Co., 1970.

Yoder, John H.

A. *The Ecumenical Movement and the Faithful Church.* Scottdale: Mennonite Publishing House, 1958.
B. "Binding and Loosing," *Concern,* No. 14. Scottdale: Herald Press, 1967.
C. "A People in the World: Theological Interpretation," *The Concept of the Believers Church,* James L. Garrett, Jr., ed. Scottdale: Herald Press, 1969.
D. "The Fullness of Christ," *Concern,* No. 17, February 1969.
E. *Nevertheless: A Meditation on the Varieties and Shortcomings of Religious Pacifism.* Scottdale: Herald Press, 1971.
F. "Anabaptist Vision and Mennonite Reality," *Consultation on Anabaptist Mennonite Theology,* A. J. Klassen, ed. Fresno: Council of Mennonite Seminaries, 1972.
G. *The Legacy of Michael Sattler.* Scottdale: Herald Press, 1973.
H. "Mennonite Political Conservatism: Paradox or Contradiction," *Mennonite Images: Historical, Cultural, and Literary Essays Dealing with Mennonite Issues,* Harry Loewen, ed. Winnipeg: Hyperion Press, 1980.
I. *The Priestly Kingdom.* Notre Dame, Ind.: Univ. of Notre Dame Press, 1984.
J. "Why I Don't Pay All of My Income Tax," *Gospel Herald,* Jan. 22, 1963; *The Mennonite,* Feb. 26, 1963.

The Author

Leland Harder was born in 1926 in Hillsboro, Kansas. Leland's roots in the Hillsboro area go back to his immigrant great-grandfather, who taught in the Krimmer Mennonite Brethren village of Gnadenau following the family's arrival from Russia in 1874. At different times Leland's grandfather and father taught at Tabor College, affiliated with the Mennonite Brethren Church, and at Bethel College, affiliated with the General Conference Mennonite Church.

Leland graduated from Bethel College (North Newton, Kan.). He then taught high school in the nearby Mennonite community of Moundridge. Awarded a research fellowship at Michigan State University, he earned an M.S. in sociology and anthropology and while there received a call into Christian ministry.

Following seminary training in Chicago, where he met and married Bertha Fast, Leland was pastor of the First Mennonite Church of Chicago for five years. He then entered a doctoral program in sociology of religion at Northwestern University, after which he and Bertha joined the faculty of Mennonite Biblical Seminary (Elkhart, Ind.).

After twenty-five years of seminary teaching, Leland and Bertha retired to North Newton, Kansas. There Leland teaches an adult Sunday school class at the Bethel College Church and works on writing, preaching, speaking, and family history. Leland is associate director of the Church Membership Profile Research Project, which gathered data reported by Leo Driedger and Howard Kauffman in *The Mennonite Mosaic* (Herald Press, 1992), data Leland interprets for lay members in this book.

Leland and Bertha are parents of two sons. John is a statistician at Ford Motor Company (Dearborn, Mich.), and John and wife, Julie, have two daughters. Tom is program director at Camp Friedenswald (Cassopolis, Mich.), and Tom and wife, Lois, have one daughter.